THE
ETERNAL
SEASON

*Ghosts of summers past,
present and future*

STEPHEN RUTT

Elliott&Thompson

First published 2021 by
Elliott and Thompson Limited
2 John Street
London WC1N 2ES
www.eandtbooks.com

ISBN: 978-1-78396-573-1

9 8 7 6 5 4 3 2 1

A catalogue record for this book is available from
the British Library.

Typesetting: Marie Doherty
Printed by CPI Group (UK) Ltd,
Croydon, CR0 4YY

And summer's lease hath all too short a date;
Sometime too hot the eye of heaven shines,
And often is his gold complexion dimm'd;
And every fair from fair sometime declines,
By chance or nature's changing course untrimm'd;
But thy eternal summer shall not fade,

. . .

So long as men can breathe or eyes can see,
So long lives this, and this gives life to thee.

Sonnet 18, William Shakespeare

Contents

Introduction: The Short Lease

This was supposed to be a book about warblers.

I was daydreaming about blackcaps one afternoon in late October, reliving the early summer days when their song had drifted through the hot, still air. The six species of warblers that bred near me had already headed south for winter a month earlier, and I found myself in that gap between the birding seasons of summer and winter. After the departure, before the arrival.

I felt as if I was about to enter a state of winter torpidity. My encounters with birds keep my emotions alive, ticking over; I was going to have to cling to the geese and the species still around me to stave off the dumb, dark numbness of winter. Summer is normally felt in its absence; anticipation building with every day after the winter solstice, as we claw back time out of the dark night, and as we grow confident that the festival of summer life is going to begin again. But the shortest night is still two long months away.

I imagined my blackcaps on their way to Spain. Or the willow warblers of Scandinavia that shelter behind the dykes and brochs of Shetland, on their way south to Senegal. Or sedge warblers from Suffolk on their way to South Africa. These rhythms seem ceaseless. Is the sedge warbler a bird of Africa or Suffolk? Where does it end? (With me blundering into a hedge.) It felt to me as if I never make enough of their presence here, their long summer stay that runs from April to September, from when they first return to the moment of their departure: the high point between the miracles of migration. I resolved there and then that their summer would be mine too. I would bear witness to it.

As I wandered down the River Nith, the hawthorns were laden with an exceptional crop of berries, a glut surpassing those I had seen previously. The sort where you briefly stop daydreaming and think *look at those amazing berries* – a feast for any late or leftover blackcap. The hawthorn bushes themselves were shouting at me, just as in spring the chiffchaffs shout from their branches.

A stranger stopped me as I dawdled on the path, lost between the berries and my absent warblers.

'It'll be a cold winter.'

'Really?' I said.

'Aye, right enough. Look at these berries. Going to be a cold one.' He walked on, tugged by his dog straining at its leash.

I've heard variations on this theme all my life, but I've never been sold on the predictive qualities of nature. A bumper crop just means it was a good summer. Flowers gorged like gluttons on sunlight and the right rain at the right time, the presence of summer lingering like a ghost. What the next year will look like depends so much on what has just been. Shakespeare's famous sonnet gets this slightly wrong. It is not the case that summer's lease 'hath all too short a date'.[1] Summer's lease is extended, the season penetrating the deepest dark of winter in berries such as these, the crop of acorns and beechmast, the survival of mistletoe, the presences and absences of species. Shakespeare thought his lover was possessed of an eternal summer but the real thing is eternal too. To ignore the joy of summer in winter would be perverse, an act of self-denial.

I appreciate once again the web of connections that we live with, that are an integral part of our world. These rhythms cannot be isolated: I can't see just the warbler by itself, alone and separate from the hawthorn; I can't see the hawthorn alone and separate from the season, without the rain and sun that caused its crop of shining red berries. To think of either alone would be to ignore so much of importance to both. John Muir, in *My First Summer in the Sierra* (written in 1911 but referring to 1869), got it correct: 'When we try to pick out anything by itself, we find it hitched to everything else in the universe.'[2] With that, the book about warblers suddenly seemed too small. A fine choice cut, the delightful small, shy, sombre-coloured singers that announce the coming summer in scrub, wood and reeds, but not the story at hand.

Birds have always been the focus of my passion for nature and they always will be. But the summer does not belong to them alone; there is a full spectrum of life to consider that can seem largely absent from the winter months: the butterflies and dragonflies that add colour to the days; the moths that haunt the warm nights and the swooping bats that pick them off; the unforgettable arachnids and amphibians that lurk in the ignored corners. The type of summer we have can dictate which species thrive or struggle, and the effect can be felt throughout the natural world, lasting long into winter. Especially among the bird populations, which, in the sparse British fauna, are at the top of so many food chains. Our summer wildlife is the filter through which we can see what's really happening in our seasons. It's a time when nature is buzzing with activity – breeding, migration, feeding frenzies – all on show for us to see how our species are faring.

Looking closely at this long summer as a whole, though, reveals that it is no longer exactly what we expect. The rhythms and connections that hold the season and its wildlife together are changing, unravelling themselves.

George Orwell, in the year after the Second World War, wrote an essay that isn't as well-known as it should be. 'Some Thoughts on the Common Toad'[3] is perhaps an outlier in his works. It's to do with the world as I know it – the signs of the seasons and the hope of nature in spring – rather than the world of politics, class struggle and war that he is more usually associated with. This, he accepts, will bring him some conflict: mentioning nature 'is liable to bring me abusive letters' from readers who think he should stick to the serious political journalism. Yet I love it. I love anything that will talk about Persephone and toads and a kestrel by Deptford gasworks with equal reverence and attention. It seems to me to be as serious as anything else he wrote.

Orwell's conclusion is worth keeping in mind:

I have always suspected that if our economic and political problems are ever really solved, life will become simpler instead of more complex, and that the sort of pleasure one gets from finding the first primrose will loom larger than the sort of pleasure one gets from eating an ice to the tune of a Wurlitzer. I think that by retaining one's childhood love of such things as trees, fishes, butterflies . . . toads, one makes a peaceful and decent future a little more probable.[4]

My heart soared when I first read that. It felt similar to Muir's hitched universe of things. Here was Orwell making a statement of the importance of nature in the future of things, as urgent as politics.

The only problem is that I'm no longer certain his assertion is true. I retained my childhood love of nature. Only 'peaceful and decent' feels further away than ever. Everything is loaded with complexity in this time of climate change and mass extinction. Nothing is simple any more. A bird you look at is no longer just a bird but one of an interlinked series of forces, capable of being expressed as statistics, that explain the terribly restless, indecent state of the world.

I have always taken a delight in the rhythms and connections of nature. The tides, the times of dawn and dusk, and all those other reminders of our place in the infinite universe. Migration and the year's annual ebb and flow of life from hemisphere to hemisphere, region to region, the dictation of time and food and habitat. But it seems to me the greatest of these rhythms, here on this island off the northwest corner of Europe, is that of the seasons: the artefact of earth's annual 365-day, 940-million-kilometre spin around the sun. Or, more specifically, the angle of rotation of the earth's axis as we make this journey. You know this, but it bears repeating: the most obvious way we know we're circling around space tipped to one side is the way our summer is so obviously, joyously not winter.

Or, at least, it should be.

In 2019 Dumfries had February days as warm as August. August held days as cold as February. Butterflies and bats were out in winter. I wore my cold-weather coat in the height of summer, my T-shirts in winter. The easy, obvious distinctions, those things we use without thinking to define the year, appear to be changing. Everything seems to be becoming fractured, fragmentary. Now I am thinking about summer and I am no longer sure what summer means.

Our way of splitting up our seasons has always been a little arbitrary. The Met Office defines four seasons but then offers two dates for when they begin: a meteorological and astronomical way of knowing. In Japan I read they have 24 seasons and 72 microseasons. In Ancient Egypt they had just three. The Gaelic cultures of Scotland, Ireland and the Isle of Man hold festivals such as Imbolc and Beltane, feasts between the solstice and the equinox, a different way of marking the passing of time. Wales has Calan Mai and Calan Gaeaf, its own versions of these.

What is not arbitrary is that our perceptions of what the seasons should be are increasingly being challenged.

My favourite sentence in a nature book belongs to
J. A. Baker: 'The hardest of all to see is what is really there.'[5]
It particularly resonates for me in the discrepancy between
the surface appearance and the actual state of nature. You
could walk into a wood on a summer's day, pretty and green,
and not know a thing was wrong if you didn't know the signs
to look for. And nowhere is that gap between appearance
and reality more apparent than with climate change – the
great invisible force holding the world to ransom.

I was eight months old when the Union of Concerned
Scientists published an open letter signed by 1,700 scientists.
It was titled 'A Warning to Humanity' and its first sentence
cautioned that 'human beings and the natural world are on
a collision course.'[6] Foresight is woven through it. Climate,
mass extinction, forests, water, the oceans are all listed,
explained, and warned about. It is clear-sighted on the
industrialised world that has caused a problem predominantly affecting innocent people. It is still extremely relevant,
which might be the most terrifying thing about it.

I don't know how old I was when I first found out about
global warming – I suspect five or six – but I remember
exactly where I was. Sprawled out, bored on the pale carpet
of my granny's living room in her Lincolnshire village. I was
an adventurous and voracious reader at a young age. I picked
up a copy of *The Times* from her magazine rack and spread
it out. Thin paper, loose ink, broad sheets. At the time there
were two words in a headline that I didn't recognise, and I
pestered my parents until they were explained to me: Kyoto
and Protocol. The Kyoto Protocol was a United Nations

initiative signed by eighty-four countries. They essentially stated that climate change is real and we are causing it.

A few years later I remember picking up a book about the greenhouse effect from the school library, thinking it might have something to do with plants and therefore nature. Instead I learned how we were cooking the planet. These things didn't shock or trouble me overly at that age. They were just facts to be remembered, and internalised.

Because I learned about it when I was young, I've never needed to discover climate change, have my own reckoning, my own realisation about my awareness and contribution to it. It's just always been a fact of life for me, as it is for the generation after mine: Greta Thunberg and the kids on climate strike, growing up with climate change and its effects as a fact of life. In the same way that no bird is just a bird any more, no sunny summer's day is just pleasant weather; it comes freighted with anxiety for our destabilised planet.

One of the side effects of the British obsession with our flora and fauna is that we have been writing about it for a long time, and have amassed a vast wealth of almanacs, calendars and diaries, stories from decades past – all of which are fascinating to read now. They are almost emissaries from the past, that 'foreign country' as L. P. Hartley had it, where 'they do things differently'.[7] They saw different things, heard different things, had different ideas. These records show us how far things have changed. Charles St John's description of corncrakes singing in the Highland night and Flora Thompson's nightingale that sang for six weeks in her Hampshire garden were ordinary things, not the sort of special moment, the crowning high point of the summer they would be for me, for so many of us, nowadays. I read the observations of old nature writing as an archive of loss. And we have lost so much. Their lists of species seen have become a litany of ghosts.

In 1962, less than twenty years after Orwell was writing about toads, came Rachel Carson's legendary *Silent Spring*. It begins with a famous apocalyptic vision of nature. A landscape without birds: Carson's 'spring without voices'.[8] This is still a fear we face for the future. While apocalyptic visions such as Carson's are vivid and powerful, perhaps they are also misleading. A silent landscape is not the only thing we should fear. The worst catastrophes come in increments, not as a sudden apocalypse. They begin with a creeping strangeness, a delicate series of disorientations that can be ignored while some birds still sing, while nature still has some voice. It's the wrong birds singing at the wrong time. The voice corrupted. It's those out of sync with time, season, country, continent . . .

Everything is now a warning: things out of order or things passing as normal that betray how far from normal we have strayed. Perhaps the eternal summer of Shakespeare's compliment has become the curse of our future.

Light, abundance, adaptation, disarray, decay. This is what I'll set out to find in my season of discovery, tracing out summer as it begins, peaks and descends. It is my way of making real what is happening, as we circle the sun; my way of working out what the warblers are really telling me about the world, and why that has a lot to do with animals that aren't warblers and with the weather that is getting hotter, drier, cooler, wetter. It is my venture into the overwhelming specificity of things and the single great threat that underpins everything.

A universal overview of summer wildlife would be impossible. Any attempt to write that would end up like the empire in Jorge Luis Borges's story that creates a 1:1 scale map of its territory, lost in its own representation rather than living in reality. So it is partial to my own view of the world (which is divided between the southwest corner of Scotland and my family in the east of England) and the places that I travel, the weather that happens to be around on that day and the species I find. I think I'm a good naturalist, but a large part of being a good naturalist is knowing what you know and your limits. So I apologise in advance to the myriad orders of the natural world including, but not limited to, plants, bumblebees, fish, mammals, bugs and beetles; your omission is my own ignorance, not a lack of importance.

And then Muir's universe of hitches comes back to bite me again. I am writing about a scenario that feasibly leads to the end of the world as we know it and then another – this damned pandemic – happens. I have an internet browser tab open with the rising numbers of infections and deaths, seeing the geographical spread of it. With the rise and spread of the virus, comes the rise and spread of anxiety. It follows me everywhere. It's in the way it occupies my every waking thought. It's in the way that I worry about needing to go to the supermarket tomorrow because we have no food and this is no longer a simple, safe act. It's in the way it has cancelled everything I have planned. Covid-19 has stolen away my spring and replaced it with a miasma of panic. Both my partner and I are medically vulnerable people. Both of us have vulnerable family and friends. Coronavirus feels far more worrying than global warming, the danger more immediate. It is something that flips the script I expected to find – that we worry about what we see. Now the enemy is something even more invisible than our carbon emissions, although its unsettling effects are clear: the Colosseum in Rome empty instead of crawling with tourists, Hebridean village halls decked out like military field hospitals, the sacked shelves of suburban supermarkets. Perhaps it's that and not the microscopic world of bacteria and viruses that worries us, more than any numbers of graphs and charts could.

This was supposed to be a book where I went out into summer, to engage with the season and see the effects of our rapidly changing climate. Nature's Colosseum not crawling with birds, butterflies, dragonflies ... Obviously in a time of pandemic this is not possible. It raises another question. The future will, I suspect, require a revival of a sort of faith or trust or the ability to appreciate a place or species deeply without feeling the need to see it or experience it directly. This is, after all, part of the reason why literature and art exist, the sharing of second-hand experiences: the sort that kindles empathy for people, animals, places. Dan Richards, while writing *Outpost*, talks of the impossible beauty of Svalbard, the Norwegian Arctic archipelago, and then the conflict he felt while writing about it – the sharing of an incredible experience that he didn't feel it was responsible to encourage. He likens this to a gourmand talking of delicious food – and then saying how you can't have any of it. But perhaps this is the medicine we need: a revival of the ability to appreciate at a distance.

But the story begins before all of this. It begins in the middle of a mess of our own making.

Rising Damp

I'm standing in the car park at Caerlaverock National Nature Reserve, looking out at the grey Solway Firth as the day dissolves at its dismal end. Water is everywhere, pooling further up the brown merse than it usually reaches. And the wetland is more water than land.

I am not alone. I overhear a conversation by the boot of a car.

'I've never seen it so wet. Global warming . . . huh . . . so they say. I dunno.'

Wetness is one of the counterintuitive risks of a changing climate. It seems to be hardwired into the mind of the general public – at least for the sort of man that loudly offers unsolicited opinions in car parks – that warm weather means dry and cold means wet. The logic could be taken that global warming means we will get drier weather. The only problem is, it's not true.

Climatologists from the University of East Anglia discovered that between 1961 and 2006 the UK got wetter in winter and that this was particularly so in Scotland and northwest England. This wasn't an increase of the number of rainy days but in the intensity of rainy days.[1] Summer is drier but they did note that 'the very wet summer of 2012 reminds us that not all summers will be dry in a warmer world.'[2] I vividly remember that summer standing under a tree at Minsmere while 70 mm of rain was dumped on my head in an hour, with lightning striking the other end of the reserve. I was completely sodden through, yet in awe of an English summer storm that held more water than I thought was possible. The warming climate is charging the system with more energy and more water vapour and the rest is inevitable.

Here on the Inner Solway the water comes from both rainfall and from the estuary's tides. The firth collects the threads of many rivers and burns and spools them into a vast Irish Sea-ward flow. I spent most of the winter volunteering with reserve staff around Caerlaverock NNR, watching as the fields behind the reserve filled up with rainwater, and how the ditches and streams that flow into the Solway fill up, then break free of their borders, flooding regularly. On a human scale the reserve is only a thin piece of land, backed by farmers' fields, somewhere between hinterland and wetland, but it is actually huge: mostly mud and saltmarsh, estuary and riverbed, and it is deeply prone to the vicissitudes of water.*

For what spends the summer here, on the Inner Solway, water is vitally important. There are ponds, which we scrutinised all winter, that are perched precariously on the merse edge, within the reach of the strongest tides. These are for natterjack toads to breed. The saltmarsh is home to waders. Behind the

---

* 8,184 hectares. To put this into context, it is the same size as the Hebridean island of Benbecula. Or, in the obligatory comparison of scale, Caerlaverock NNR is the size of 20,223 football pitches.

sea wall, the reedbed is where more birds attempt to breed. The habitat here is a delicate interplay of factors: each is shaded by the amount of water it holds, the amount of salt it is exposed to. Too much rain dilutes the salt, a breach of salty seawater curdles the freshwater marshes. Everything that grows or breeds here does so because of these very specific needs, the fine calibration of their tolerances to what water ends where. A bad winter can wreck the summer habitats of an environment such as this.

A NatureScot report into the impact of climate change on the Scottish landscape flags up the Inner Solway area – here – as being of the highest risk of damage and flooding following storm surges, when the winds push huge tides towards low coastlines with results that can be devastating. We have been recording Britain's surface sea temperature for 150 years: eight of the ten warmest years have been since 2000.[3] The Met Office – one of the last sober bastions of British life – writes on its website that the link between coastal flooding and rainfall and global warming is a 'complex' one. But it goes on to state: 'There is strong evidence that increasing sea temperatures increase the intensity of tropical storms. Rising sea levels also increase the risk of coastal flooding.'[4] Over the course of a day the Solway changes hugely but its borders have been fixed by sea walls and the hard edges of human land use. I wonder for how long it will stay this way. If, indeed, it can.

1

Summer in a Blizzard

M igration. The theory is grand, as theory always is.
It goes like this. One day you wake up from your
roost. Flick your wings to the tip of the branch, the edge of
the rock face, the barn gable, and pause. The bones of the
landscape remain but the skin is changing. Your territory
is there but your food is not and there's perhaps a touch of
chill in the air. The nights are lengthening. Time is running
short.

So you flick your wings again. Some of you wait until
hidden by night, some brave the flight by day, all feel the
rush of air beneath feathers and . . . keep feeling it. Keep
feeling it until you're somewhere south of this island, this
continent, this hemisphere.

New warmth. New food. Until it begins to happen again,
a few months later. Time slips. Food disappears. Days are
shortening. An impulse fires inside your baked-bean-sized
brain. And you launch yourself off your branch, rock, gable,
heading back north. As you have been doing all your life,
as your species has been doing since the end of the last Ice
Age, ten to fifteen thousand years ago, returning with the
advent of summer. So what happens when this begins to
go wrong?

When the birds have begun to steal a march on summer, it means we need to as well. To see what this disruption to migration means, we need to begin before the traditional spring arrival. We must begin in the dark depths of winter.

My plan was scotched by a delayed train.

I was having a slow month, my brain beached on banks of lethargy, in the depths of dark January. I'd decided to kick-start it by heading to see an old friend, Stephen Menzie, on the very edge of Liverpool. He would ring some birds in his garden and I would watch his hands delicately holding small bodies, taking measurements and manipulating a ring over a twig-thin leg, while the weather was good. Then we'd catch up indoors when the standard forecast of this month – gale-force wind and heavy rain – swept through. Instead I watched the good weather leave while sitting on a stationary train at Wigan station. By the time I made it down to Liverpool, the wind was icy, and swirling down the suburban streets. The sky threatened rain. The light of the morning was dwindling.

'Baltic,' I said.

'Usual,' he said.

I have known Menzie for half my life. For most of that time he has been a bird ringer. Where I am obsessed with birds, he is obsessed with what we can know about birds, the feather minutiae and how it changes with age and sex and what that means. He's always been a scientist and I am not. I know enough to identify birds. Then my brain moves towards other tangibles. Menzie knows those, of course, but he keeps knowing birds in ever greater levels of detail, and it leaves me in awe of what he can see.

Over coffee we discuss his garden birds. It is a normal-sized garden for a suburban semi-detached house. A small lawn fenced in, a single winter cherry tree, and some anonymous dark green bushes, dangling five sunflower-seed feeders hosting clusters of greenfinches. It seems to do well for birds, he says, despite being nothing special. He's spent long enough looking to know exactly what is out there.

I have a mouthful of coffee when Menzie gasps. He gives directions. It's in the mahonia, it's in the bare branches in front of the mahonia, it's in the ornamental cherry. A blackcap. A small warbler, its body as dull grey-brown as the day. It is a female – a *browncap*, instead of a blackcap* – and this was the cause of his reaction. Traditionally a summer visitor, blackcaps have been increasingly wintering in the UK, and Menzie has been watching the same male blackcap in his garden all winter – but this is the first female, an unexpected sign of change. And anything new is exciting to a birder. His quick eyes had spotted, identified and noticed that it wasn't the regular blackcap before I'd even begun to look in the right direction.

Now we are both captivated by this small sensation of summer in deep winter. The blackcap hides well in the pale pink blossom of the ornamental cherry against the leaden sky. Against the sharp-leaved mahonia it stands out, paler

---

* The blackcap is one of those species that has a rather sexist name, referring exclusively to the male and bearing no resemblance to the female.

than the dark green foliage or dense black shadows. It pokes the yellow spike of mahonia flowers with its bill before flitting off, over the fence, gone with the weather.

Rain begins to fall. We don't see the blackcap again.

Summer in winter. Perhaps this needs a more dramatic example to make the point, because migration is changing and not just in suburban blackcaps.

A few Februarys ago I was in Cornwall with my partner Miranda when the storm that the press called 'the beast from the east' struck. We were about to head out for the day, not believing the forecast, when we watched the sky turn from blue to pewter, and what we expected to fall as rain fell as snow. So instead we walked to the next village, marvelling at the speed with which the world turned white. The postman walking past in shorts said, 'I haven't seen snow in thirty years here', and when the sun came out, the local children flinging loose handfuls of snow at each other made that perfectly clear.

How birds react to snow differs depending on the species. The gulls in the lee of the harbour stuck it out, as they would with any familiar Atlantic storm. The smaller birds were frantic.

Whenever I'd walked this area before I hadn't seen many birds down the tight winding alleys between the small walled gardens of the houses, but now they were everywhere and busy, foraging with the mania of staying alive, their fear temporarily put aside. There was a firecrest in someone's bay tree, a redwing hunched by a doorstep – and a chiffchaff foraging, scurrying in plant pots like a mouse between soil and greenery.

A chiffchaff in a blizzard. Summer in a snowstorm. I can't overstate how bizarre it seemed. This summer visitor is the species that more than any other fires the starting gun on the season. It belongs in a sunlit woodland or a green hedgerow buzzing with easy life. It was almost uncanny, seeing everything in the wrong place, birds shuffled like a pack of cards and dealt into strange locations by the harsh hand of the weather.

For the remainder of our short, snow-bound stay in Cornwall I saw a chiffchaff every day in an unexpected place. On the harbour wall, in a flower bed, flitting around a pampas-grass bush with the sea as a background, gulls for neighbours.

Blackcap: *Sylvia atricapilla*. Chiffchaff: *Phylloscopus collybita*. Two warblers that are quite unlike each other, yet, according to the old textbooks, they share a key trait. They are both common summer warblers of the UK, migrating to the Mediterranean for winter sun and food, returning in March or April to sing in the spring.

Sylvia: from the Latin for 'wood'; it shares an etymology with 'sylvan', which gets something of the essence of warblers – sprite-like essences of the countryside, hedgerows, scrub and trees. *Phylloscopus*: from the Greek for 'leaf-seeker'. If the *Sylvia* warblers are of trees and bushes, then the

Phylloscopus warblers go deeper into the trees and bushes, lurking, flitting in the branches, behind the screen of leaves where they glean their food. While the *Sylvia* can be quite striking-looking birds, the *Phylloscopus* are all variations on a theme of chlorophyll with yellow highlights; adept at hiding in their world of leaf-filtered light.

The blackcap and its sister species the garden warbler are unusual. Their common ancestor split off roughly 13 million years ago from the other *Sylvia* warblers. Where the blackcap and the garden warbler stayed sombrely plumaged, the other *Sylvia*s evolved pinks and reds, moustachial stripes and eye-rings. The blackcap and the garden warbler might not be much to look at, but they share a similar rich song, suggesting it is akin to that of their common ancestor. When spring rolls around, the prehistoric effervescence of this song fills the air, coming from hedgerows, dense gardens, small woods.

Palaeo-ornithologists have found fossils of blackcaps from the Pleistocene. This island belonged to birds well before it belonged to Cheddar Gorge Man. Richard Smyth, in a sentence I find both moving and poignant, has written that 'no human was ever born into a birdless world'.[1] And no human has ever lived in a world without the buoyant melody of blackcap song, the chiffchaff shouting its name over and over. Because of this, to me, birds operate on two scales of time. On the one hand, species are impossibly old, literal living dinosaurs, often barely changing. And on the other hand, individual birds are so vitally alive in the present, living fast, singing beautifully, raising their broods and dying young – and it is all over so quickly. The scale of the species is almost geological in breadth; the scale of the individual is the gap it flits between from branch to branch. This regularly leaves me awestruck.

To which of these scales does migration – one of the great rhythms of the natural world – belong? Migration is genetically encoded within birds, the young of which often head out alone, at night, with no training, no guide, on their journey. The example ornithology gives has a familiar origin: 'Within a single species (e.g. blackcap), the entire range, from complete sedentariness to long-distance migratoriness can be found. The fact that these extremes are present within single species demonstrates that migratory adaptations are highly flexible in an evolutionary sense.'[2] Perhaps the answer is that migration belongs to both rhythms. We are witnessing not a glitch but a modern response to a changing world, reinforced by each breeding season. What starts with a few brave individuals breaking the mould gradually becoming an established pattern.

That might explain a blackcap in Liverpool in January. A chiffchaff in a February blizzard. They weren't the first examples of their species adapting their routines, abandoning what should be an easier life in gentler climates of a Mediterranean winter. But they were the most extreme examples I had seen. Witnessing the world change in front of you can be a jarring experience.

There are some facts about bird migration that bear repeating. Birds can navigate by the sun and the night sky. To do that, they must also have an awareness of time, and an understanding of how time affects the movement of the sun or stars across the sky.

This was discovered in 1949 in Germany by Gustav Kramer, who placed a blackcap in a cage under the night sky. (*Sylvia* warblers always migrate at night.) Migratory animals in captivity are known to exhibit what is known as 'zugunruhe' – literally meaning 'migratory restlessness' – when unable to follow their urge to move. Kramer noticed that the zugunruhe of his blackcaps was also oriented in the direction they should be migrating in.

It is something that is genetically encoded and specific to certain populations. Birds prefer not to migrate over large bodies of water, and the path of blackcaps from southwest Germany is the same as those from Britain: they move to the southwest, travelling to Spain or North Africa. Those from eastern Austria are genetically disposed to head the other way, over the Balkans, across Turkey, down through the Middle East and into East Africa, all to avoid a sea crossing and ending up in the middle of the Sahara.[3]

But whether the birds currently wintering in suburban Liverpool should be in the Costa del Sol or a date-palm plantation in Morocco is not the important point here. What's more interesting, in terms of changing migratory patterns, is that the blackcap in Menzie's garden was almost certainly not born in Britain.

Ringing is the best tool for knowing what we have. The most incontrovertible and bird-friendly way of working out movements from A to B, while also enabling us to know how old the birds are, their sex, their weight, their condition. Whether they're doing well or not. Ringing is great at telling us what's exactly in front of us. It reveals the blackcaps you would never have seen. The problem is what it doesn't tell us. If the bird has never been caught before, it won't tell us where it has come from. Or if the individual is never caught again, it won't say where it went. Or if it is caught again, how it got there; ringing will only ever draw straight lines on maps. It's a blunt tool for knowing, but currently still the best we've got. From the data, it is possible to work out some extraordinary things.

A theory was developed in the 1970s by D. R. Langslow, from the accumulated recoveries of ringed blackcaps. By plotting where and when they were ringed and recovered, he was able to calculate rough dates for when British-born blackcaps were present in the country, and when they had migrated, and when blackcaps born elsewhere in Europe were present, migrating through the coastal bird observatories of Britain. He was not able to find a record of a blackcap here in winter that had been ringed here in the summer.[4] It seems that while our summer visitors, the British birds, are continuing with their usual migration to winter in the Mediterranean, the German birds have started to change route, coming instead to our shores.

Wintering blackcaps had been first noticed in the nineteenth century. A survey followed only in the 1950s, with the tentative note in the results summary that 'during the winter it can be seen that the blackcaps readily change their feeding habits', going on to list bread, meat bones, kitchen scraps.[5]

This rich winter diet has become bird seed and suet fat balls as garden bird feeding has grown in popularity. It seems to be an important factor in helping these blackcaps survive the British winter, with a British Trust for Ornithology leaflet about blackcaps speculating that this is the reason why wintering blackcaps can be quite 'bolshie' with other birds around the feeders.[6]

The only thing is whether observation backs that up. Menzie says that the blackcaps in his garden have always been on the mahonia, the azalea or occasionally around the catkins of the ornamental hazel. 'We've got a few apples strewn around the garden, the seed feeders and the fat balls, and every blackcap in the garden has always ignored them. It's odd.'

There is a landmark book called *Sylvia Warblers*. It is an outstanding work of scholarship, of laser-focused intensity on the genus: everything that one could possibly ever need to know, and a fair amount of things one wouldn't. After its discussion of blackcaps in the British winter, it suggests:

> This begs the question, of course, why UK-breeding blackcaps appear not to have noticed that they might remain year-round. Probably this is only a matter of time: if the current climatic trend continues, the UK blackcap population may become partially migratory, with steadily more birds remaining throughout the year.[7]

If. The book was written in 2001 and the question remains open, despite the climatic trends continuing. In the meantime, this population of German blackcaps that spend the winter in Britain are beginning to show differences. They are returning to Germany at a different time from those that still carry out the classic Mediterranean-bound migration, meaning they are no longer interbreeding. Their genes are becoming isolated: the driving force behind what makes a new species. Their beaks are narrower – better for bird feeders or foraging in mahonia flowers. Their wings are rounder, losing the length needed for longer migrations. They have browner backs – I don't know why. But by feeding garden birds, combined with our warming climate, we are literally altering species. We are witnessing evolution in action, adapting to what we've made of the world.[8]

I leave Liverpool slowly, courtesy of another delayed train, half an hour standing on a platform and then an unexpected bus replacement service, while the weather went from repellent to repulsive. It feels like a testament to their tenacity – blackcap or chiffchaff – that some have given up on winters in warmer, drier places for a season of this (and I really can't overemphasise how unpleasant this winter, this day, has been). Although it's actually nothing to do with tenacity. If it were, they would all be doing it; they would all have been doing it forever. It's not that birds are getting tougher. The climate is changing, and although this day, this winter, might be appalling, the overall trend is enabling the flexibility built into their migratory mechanisms. And with each passing season those changes are reinforced genetically by every successful migration.

I get a text from Menzie a few weeks later. The male blackcap that we didn't see that day had discovered the fat balls in his garden and spent the rest of the day on them. For just one day only – it hasn't returned to them since. Proving the rule that you can only observe, never generalise.

The world is full of amazing things. Take the willow warbler, *Phylloscopus trochilus*. Although chiffchaff are common they tend to fade out to the north. Willow warblers carry on being common all the way through to the north of Russia – and to its farthest eastern edge as well – in huge numbers. BirdLife estimates there's between 400 million and 645 million of them in the world, a staggering number of small green and yellow warblers. Individually they weigh 10 grams and measure 11 cm from bill to tail. A study of migratory American warblers – unrelated to European warblers but similar enough to bear comparison – found that they needed to eat 1.2–1.7 times their own bodyweight in insect larvae each day to get the calories they needed.[9] If you average out the numbers, take the low end of the population estimate, you end up with 6,000 tonnes of larvae a day needed to sustain that population. Maths escapes me at the best of times, but the takeaway is that the world's willow warblers need a lot of caterpillars to survive.

What we get for that – our reward for keeping the ecosystems of the northern hemispheres functioning – is a cascade of song. A silvery whistle of notes descending the musical scale. It is a glorious song, somehow sounding both sad and joyful.

But while the willow warbler's contribution is beautiful, it is just one of a chorus that forms an essential heralding of the summer to come. And for me it is the simple singing of the chiffchaff that stands out and makes my heart rise. 'Chiff chaff', two words repeated like a football chant. Some get their name slightly wrong: 'silp salp' or 'chaff chiff' – all variations on the same theme.

The chiffchaff used to be the first singing migrant for most birders. But it's no longer the case. A quick search on the internet reveals that the first chiffchaff to sing in the UK in 2020 did so probably on 8 January, between a rubbish dump and a sewage farm in Dorset, although a number were heard singing in December as well. (The difference between 31 December and 1 January is lost on birds; the distinction between one year and another is an arbitrary one.) Most of the observers remarked that it was the first time they had heard a chiffchaff singing in December or January.

The effect it has on me is not produced only by the actual living bird. If I hear a recording in winter it will still transmit a little pulse of joy. The year's first singing chiffchaff will do more than that. It will give me a broad smile and make my day – despite being the same simple song every year. Similar greening hedgerows always appear empty of life until the bushes begin to shout. But if it's available all year round, will that association last? Or will that jolt of excitement, the anticipation that the warmer months are on their way, gradually disappear?

I return to Gilbert White. He liked blackcaps – famously writing that their song was 'a sweet, wild note'.[10] His record-keeping meant he could date the returning of his blackcaps, very precisely to the end of the second week of April and that (in 1767) they were 'never seen in winter'.[11] If White were around today he would be disturbed by the fact that he could now find them in any season. That the arrival of his local breeding blackcaps would now be a month earlier. He might be beset by a sudden uncertainty as to whether a blackcap was an early returning British bird or a late departing German bird. His calendar of certainties, his almanac, his knowledge of natural history would be thrown into disarray. Everything disconnected.

Gilbert White was a precise man. His dating of the arrival of blackcaps isn't the faux precision of a man who might make an outrageous prediction. His powers of observation, of studying birds from life and not from books or the theories of others, were strong enough for him to write in a letter to naturalist Thomas Pennant in 1768, 'I make no doubt but there are three species of the willow-wrens', meaning chiffchaff, willow warbler and wood warbler. Differentiating between them as 'songster' and 'chirper', he sketches out the basic differences in size, song, legs and time of singing. Of the chiffchaff, he notes, 'The chirper (being the first summer-bird of passage that is heard, the wryneck* sometimes excepted)

---

* Extinct now as a breeding bird in Britain other than in exceptionally rare, irregular circumstances. The wryneck is a migratory woodpecker with an incredible bark-like camouflage plumage.

begins his two notes in the middle of March.'[12] Without binoculars he was able to notice and describe the fine distinctions that create the visual boundaries between species. I can't imagine what it would be like to receive this as a letter, to have your understanding of a bird totally upended, one species turned into three. Without binoculars, if a *Phylloscopus* warbler flits in front of me, I don't even bother trying to identify it. But then we can't all be as good as White was.

If you see a *Phylloscopus* in the wrong season it is almost certainly a chiffchaff. Chiffchaffs have been spending the winter in Britain for longer than blackcaps have. In Howard Saunders' early twentieth-century *Manual of British Birds*, he doesn't mention blackcaps in winter, whereas he says chiffchaffs can spend the winter in the climate of Cornwall and Devon. In the British Trust for Ornithology's most recent *Atlas of British Birds* (comprised of four years of surveying, a century after Saunders') chiffchaffs are present in winter throughout England, with only sporadic gaps, south of a line between Lancashire and Lincolnshire.

This is not the case with the willow warbler. Despite their similarity to chiffchaffs they are a very different species, still very much a bird that comes for our summers, unable for whatever reason to handle our winters. But there are, already, credible sightings of willow warblers in January. Not many but enough to suggest that if things carry on as they are, they'll be next, ready to exploit a milder winter that holds more insects.

I don't know yet if the willow warbler's gently melancholic melody can replace the two-note shout of a chiffchaff in my heart as the sign that winter is over, the warmer months on their way. Even if it can, perhaps by that time they'll be wintering here too. This is the problem with writing about the future: by the time you find out if you're right, you're too late. This matters to me, in a way that is not just nostalgia. A book about summer wildlife shouldn't begin on a cold day in January in a suburb of Liverpool or in a February blizzard in Cornwall.

It may be too obvious to say that White wouldn't recognise the countryside nowadays, 232 years on from his *Natural History of Selbourne*. There is a word for what he would feel: 'solastalgia'. It was coined in 2007 by the eco-philosopher Glenn Albrecht for the feeling of pain that comes with environmental loss, and how it rebounds onto a loss of identity. Or in Albrecht's words, 'Solastalgia is a form of homesickness one gets when one is still at "home".'[13] This disorientation of the seasons, the sudden lack of 'normal' in what was once, reliably, predictably, boringly ordinary. The solastalgia of Gilbert White is one of nature no longer making sense: the species of summer in winter.

There is a thing called seasonal lag. That is, the delayed effect between the earth's position in its orbit of the sun and the weather we get. It's why February is often the coldest month, a month and a bit after the shortest day, when in the north we are at our maximum tilt away from the sun. We are inching closer to the beginning of summer, even if the weather doesn't seem to reflect that, even if the chiffchaffs and blackcaps have stuck it out with us, offering that scintilla of summer in the bleak dreich winter.

The unexpected visitors help a little. It's the surprise of the present and the promise of the species of summer to come. But then it troubles me. It is part of the world that is getting weirder, that old familiar order of things that no longer seems quite so set and ordered and reliable. These new migration patterns are clear signs of a world that is changing around us in real time. And it's happening more quickly than we can get used to it.

First Swallow

I am sitting in the sun, thinking, and through a deep blue, cloudless sky, the first swallow of the year comes sailing. It is singing as if to itself – of all the land covered since last September, all the sky flitted through since it was last here. Its tail is a long extension of its elegant, long, thin body and the quick flickering of those wings. And it's off, over the hedge, into the hamlet in an instant.

One swallow doesn't make a summer. It's one of those clichés that everyone knows: the origin of it, from Aristotle's *Nicomachean Ethics*, is less widely known. The full context of the quote is: 'For one swallow does not make a summer, nor does one day; and so too one day, or a short time, does not make a man blessed and happy.'[1] That suggests to me that the swallow was well known already: familiar enough to be used in common example. I guess in Ancient Greece they still had freak spring storms, or the cold days when the flow of warm southern air ushering migrant birds up from Africa would swing to the north and the season – and its birds – would shudder to a halt.

I like this a lot: I have a tendency to go on about how birds (and our passions for them) can be used as ways of linking us to the world, its people and places, whether across the distance of space or time. This swallow – this common phrase on this fine early April day – links me to the Cape of South Africa. It links me to the inventors of Western civilisation, those first Europeans who just sat (doubtless outside on a spring day, as sunny as this one) and thought and saw swallows and knew what they were and enjoyed them.

2

The Lengthening Light

We require light.

Light is like time. It is always changing but the pace is too slow to notice until suddenly, one evening it is light when you leave work, or one morning, you wake up with day leaking in at the curtain's edge. It is there, unlike yesterday. And you realise with a jolt of surprise – is that the time of the year?

Light is the trigger. Energy abounds. Sap runs under skin again. All that pent-up energy from winter's dark coop bursts out.

Light is a substance that cannot be contained or controlled. The impact it makes is profound, yet hard to measure. As it lengthens our days, the year progresses into April, the month of change, of movement. The first half belongs in spirit to March, the second half to May and all the time between is a time of greening and arrivals.

I don't want to say we wake up again with the light because that's not quite true. Dormancy is not sleep, it's more like an exhibition of patience. The bony tree in winter is not dead or asleep but waiting, sensing the forthcoming shifts in light and warmth, waiting for the right moment for the leaves to force their way through the buds again. It is known as budburst – that moment when the leaf, tightly wrapped up in itself, breaks through the bud, then unfurls vividly, as if it's the tree's first breath again.

It's the same as me, sitting patiently by the window, not dormant but not at my best, waiting for spring to grab me and shake me back into working order again. I'm waiting for my own budburst.

It begins with blackthorn painting its bright white blossom straight on to twigs while the hawthorn finds its leaves. The hawthorn then flares into blossom while the blackthorn leaves emerge. It will end with the willow smoking its seeds into the air, aimlessly drifting, guided by the breeze. In the middle, the horse chestnut – an introduced species from the Balkans that feels quintessentially English to me – will flower in big candles of white and pink before burning up early in the height of summer, its leaves eaten from the inside out by the larvae of the horse chestnut leaf-miner moth.

We are not there yet. But we are creaking back into motion. We begin again.

Days of sunshine after rain. The sense that spring, a verb after all, was finally doing things, although it feels more like midsummer than March. We're having lunch in the garden with six species of butterflies and three species of bumblebee.* The leafless apple trees look dead in the heat and I

---

* Early bumblebee, common carder bee and buff-tailed bumblebee. The butterflies were: peacock, brimstone, small white, holly blue, comma and

have to remind myself of the month. The ash and the horse chestnut are budding, their thick black and brown bulbous tips are ready to burst green.

We're in Bedfordshire with Miranda's family. We'd come down for a visit amid the rising intensity of the coronavirus pandemic, and it felt as if we were the only people heading south. There are pleas from the Highlands and Islands and parts of Wales for visitors and second-home owners not to come north. The next day the country entered lockdown and we are stuck in Bedfordshire.

Despite the heat, I feel chilled to the core and deeply anxious. I have picked up a copy of the novel *Harvest* by Jim Crace, in which he writes of the plague: 'Contagion is known to be a crafty passenger, a stowaway.'[1] A line that stands out. Covid-19 is sticky. This and its invisibility means that anything could be carrying it. The advice is to wash your hands and now every time I pass a sink I feel the need to do so. It becomes like a new ritual. For twenty seconds, I become deeply aware of the simple action that was once carried out on autopilot. Aware of each fold of flesh in my fingers and the exact expanse of my palms, any surface to which the virus could cling. I don't like being aware of my body. The luxury of being a young, mostly healthy, white male is that I can completely ignore myself and carry on. The virus upends that. Mostly healthy: I become keenly conscious of my rubbish lungs. In normal times I just carry my

small tortoiseshell. There were also bee flies and hairy-footed flower bees around the Pulmenaria.

inhalers with me and go about my normal life. There is no normal life now.

We are advised against all non-essential travel. The TV shows pictures of police forces across the country stopping drivers, turning around those that they deem as carrying out non-essential journeys. Derbyshire police dye a picturesque lagoon black to deter visitors and broadcast drone footage of dog-walkers. It feels like a bad dream of authoritarianism.

I cannot visit the woodlands and forests across the country as I had planned to at the start of the year. But this won't stop me from tracking the changing light through the awakening trees. There is no shade of green on earth as bright and luminous as the light through a fresh leaf.

I make do with what's around locally, and walk to the local wood, a small wood, nestled at the bottom of a dip in the land, behind the next village. It is old: the outline of a medieval fishpond complex is preserved by the path that loops around a series of stagnant ponds, lined with willow and alder, the water-loving trees. It is a good wood: mostly deciduous and deep, thick with its own wild growth, not overly neatened. The air here has that mulchy smell, the intermingling mix of decay and fresh growth. The canopy holds no leaves yet but the understorey bushes do, as a blur of green behind the bare branches and the wood feels charged with the potential of what is to come. It's a special moment, early in the year, when the light can reach the heart of the woodland without interruption.

It helps that this is a good wood. Not all woodland is the same. There are conifer plantations all over the country, where trees are grown as crops, for their flesh is straight and hard and good for building. They are planted close to each other, where they block out the light from reaching the soil beneath, which is anyway hidden under a springy pile of conifer needles. They are dark, oppressive, unwelcoming.

We call these 'forests' just because of the density of trees, which is inaccurate. The historical meaning of forest is a place kept by a monarch for hunting, which goes some way to explaining why the Forest of Bowland in Lancashire is mostly moorland. But nobody uses the word this way any more. Now that forest just means a large wooded area, it lets these tree farms masquerade as something that might occur naturally. In these conifer plantations it's only the limited wildlife that can survive in them and the temperature that gives you an idea of the season. Summer, there, is reduced to a skeleton of itself.

The sole exception to the seasonal monotony is the larch tree: a conifer that loses its needles like a deciduous tree and in spring produces flowers that look like upside-down pink pineapples. They are the earliest British tree to bud-burst. These are the only things in their favour: they were the original mass-farmed tree – introduced in the eighteenth century to Blair Atholl in Perthshire as a source of timber, and indirectly responsible for the rise of bad, dark conifer plantations across the country. Wordsworth hated larch trees, describing their summer appearance as having a 'dingy, lifeless hue'.[2] Which is perhaps harsh, as it is no duller a shade of dark green than other plantation pines. But he railed against their proliferation in Cumbria, with the memorable line: 'I . . . regret that they should have selected these lovely vales for their vegetable manufactory.'[3] It's one of the few things Wordsworth and I will agree about.

Deciduous woods are a different matter: the opposite of dingy and lifeless. Oak trees buzz with light and life in a way that is not always visible to the human eye. If planting a tree is an act of faith in the future, then observing a tree is also an act of faith: I trust the dendrologists, the ecologists, the entomologists and the mycologists who can discern the life and the processes happening behind the bark, in the canopy, behind the veil of leaves and under the earth, that remain invisible to me. The Woodland Trust tells me that more life can be found in oak woodlands than any other British woodland and I have been around enough larch trees and conifer plantations not to doubt them.

Britain has two native species of oak: pedunculate and sessile, distinguished by slight differences in leaf shape and whether the acorns grow on stalks or not.* The trees themselves don't particularly care for this distinction – and they rampantly hybridise anyway† – and neither does their symbolism: the oak is one of those unfortunate things that has transcended familiarity to become part of the national

---

* A very basic guide: pedunculate leaves are deeply lobed and the acorns are on stalks. Sessile lobes are shallower and the leaf is thicker at the tip, the acorn is not on a stalk.

† The end result looking somewhere between the two species, which are already similar and highly variable anyway.

mythology. 'Heart of Oak' is the marching song of the British navy, dating back to the eighteenth century, when ships were made from the heartwood – the strongest, straightest wood in the tree – of oak. I prefer the bit where the oak tree is the heart of our woodland ecology.

Under that green oak canopy of summer, a colour that Sylvia Townsend Warner described as 'defiantly green' in a diary entry of 1949, is a lot of life.[4] In 2019, a team of scientists published a paper summarising the results of what is supported by that defiant green. It consulted 610 sources of data, finding 2,300 associated species of six major groups (birds, invertebrates, lichens, fungi, mosses and mammals).[5] Of these, 326 species are obligate – that is to say they are species without choice, species for whom it is the oak or nothing at all – and 257 of those are the invertebrates, the insects, arachnids, woodlice, snails and worms that underpin the food chain. This is just under a quarter of all the invertebrates that are associated with oak.

As well as this huge variety of life, the researchers found that the age of trees played a role. For the obligate species, the age of the tree doesn't matter. For those species that have a choice, the number of species found more than doubled in the mature and veteran oaks.

Researchers also found an association with the ash tree. The oak is associated with 1,178 species of invertebrate. The ash is associated with only 1,058 species of any type.[6] Despite this, the ash is also exceptionally important to the health of woodlands – their leaf-fall is an efficient recycler of nutrients into the soil. It was found that if the ash was lost from a woodland along with the oak, the number of imperilled species shot up compared with the number if oak alone was lost. For a wood to flourish, green and glorious with life, it must have this diversity.

The sweetness of sunlight again. This is the moment to catch woodland, while the light reaches in through the open canopy, and you can see everything without shadow, the way that the trunks and branches layer over each other like fur. I am as solar-powered as the leaves are. I don't quite photosynthesise (I would if I could), but it feels as though a similar process is happening inside me: light converted through skin to energy.

It's not just me. Scientists call this length of light 'photoperiod', and study its effect on wildlife, flora and people. Photosynthesis is linked to the sap rising in deciduous trees. In their winter dormancy, they push their sugars and waters to their roots. When spring stirs them into action, the sugar-water mix, sap, rises through the tree, supplying the tips of the branches with energy.

We've known for a long time that photoperiod makes the sap rise for birds too. Studies on a range of species have shown that exposure to light – whether natural or artificial – enlarges their testes, induces them to sing and either migrate northwards or hold a territory.[7] The word scientists like to use to describe this is 'proximate', meaning something that is immediately responsible, in contrast to 'ultimate', which is the real reason that something is made necessary.

Food is the ultimate reason for migration; light is the proximate that enables the birds to know when to migrate and sing and breed, keeping their impulses in time with their biological calendar.[8]

For something as nebulous as light, the effect it has on the earth is striking. As the planet warms, it would seem logical that trees could start growing further north, to make the most of new areas that would once have been too cold for them. But trees rely on photoperiod, as much as they do temperature; no matter how warm the planet gets, the amount of light a place receives is unchanging, one of a vanishingly small set of constants we have left. Budburst is controlled by a combination of light and warmth; photosynthesis requires only the light. Light is proximate for trees as well as birds.*

In two months' time, when the leaves have flourished and feasted on the light, they will lose their incredible green translucence and turn opaque and a darker shade of green with it. That is to say, while the initial rebirth of a woodland might be a carnival of life – the unfurling of colour and song after the seasons of dormancy, death and decay – there is always space for shadow. Looking up into a tree against the sky, the glimpses of light filtered through sessile oak leaves appear white. Looking down or across into a tree, where the bulk of it shades the light, the shadowed

---

* Also proximate: vernalisation, the process by which trees and flowers need to be exposed to cold temperatures in winter to stimulate vigorous growth the following summer.

gaps between branches and leaves are almost black. As the summer stretches on and the canopy closes and the leaves lose their vibrancy and become a darker green, the light that falls on a tree becomes even more extreme: white where it reaches and dark where it doesn't. The late-summer birder faces a struggle, when the woods are silent and the birds are perfectly, unexpectedly, camouflaged.

The promise of summer retreats, tantalisingly out of reach. After the spell of sunny warm weather, we get a too-cold day of strong, unsettled winds swaying the horse-chestnut branches. The garden is littered with fallen burst buds. I pick one up. It is sticky with the sugars that are coursing through the tree at this time of year. At the base of the bud is the hard, protective end that the leaves have pushed open with a force that seems impossible for a soft, flaccid leaf. If I could see where these fell from, I would see the semi-circle-shape scars with a half-moon of dots left by the leaf stem in the branch. They are supposed to look like nailed horseshoes, one potential root for the name 'horse chestnut'.[9]

There are four bunches of leaves, each flat like a hand, the individual leaves still creased and folded up the middle, long and thin as fingers, their veins deeply lined like the prints of our palms. This metaphor is partial of course. It has seven fingers (I do not) and a tan-orange downy fluff on the underside (I do not). In the middle of its four hands, a small solid spike, the stem onto which the flowers blossom, which, when fertilised, will produce an autumn bounty of conkers, and turn me into a schoolboy again, picking them up or kicking them down paths. I love the horse chestnut for this. An immigrant that has become an essential part of our countryside culture. I bring the fallen bud and leaves inside and decorate my pile of books with it for a bit.

I am coming back into myself.

In these unreal times, when it seems impossible to think of anything but the invisible sickness and its visible wreckage, the sun of southern England is baking some of the anxiety out of me and everything briefly feels all right as the brimstones – lurid lemon and lime butterflies – visit each dandelion I left in the lawn when I cut the grass.

Life under lockdown is bearable here in Bedfordshire, unexpected Bedfordshire. Better than it would be in our small Scottish flat, now that the geese are departing and all we have is our blank garden of grass that we cut only when the neighbours complain. The family garden has an ash tree, flower beds and gardening tasks (which I carry out only for the sensation of being a benevolent god to the robins who follow my every move, listening to the commandments of my trowel).*

The ash tree is usually the last species to burst. There is only one in the garden here but ash predominates in the

---

* I'm aware that the real reason they follow gardeners is that they evolved to follow wild boar, the forest's great earth turners.

hedgerows of this part of Bedfordshire. This area inverts my expectations of what tree, where. Oaks are more irregular here than anywhere else I've been; I'm not used to the frequency of ash. It gives me an opportunity to test an old country proverb: 'Oak before ash, in for a splash. Ash before oak, in for a soak.' There is no truth in it, but climate change is making it ever more unlikely that ash will burst its buds before oak. A mapping project carried out by the Woodland Trust has discovered that the oak's budburst is on average ten to sixteen days earlier than it was in 2001, whereas the ash is only one to twelve days earlier. The oak, it seems, is leaving the ash behind, adapting to our warmer climate with greater speed.

I have been tracking them over the past fortnight as the ash went from bare and bony to black-budded. It's a subtle awakening – the black hard buds that become a spray of dark-purple flowers, giving the tree a blotchy effect, which lets you identify them from the other side of a field. Meanwhile the handful of oaks that I have found here are absolutely bare. It's the slowest race I have ever seen – and I'm the only one who knows it's a race.

It happens on 12 April.* An Easter Sunday bathed in sunshine and greenery. I spot my first grass snake of the year, and I note the ash in the garden with three groups of bright green leaves gently waving. Out front, the oak in the hedge is

---

* Before we make any links between leaves, life and Easter, I should note that 12 April was the average date for British budburst in 2016, according to the Woodland Trust.

still brown and bare and unleafed. The ash in the hedgerow beyond is a vivid waving beacon of spring greenery, its leaves shaped like feathers and translucent like the tips of wings. Ash before oak. We're in for a soak.

It's the 15th before I notice the oak out front has suddenly, hurriedly, come into its green, as if making up for lost time. It's then that I go for a walk down a new path and find a fully leaved large oak tree. There are also some smaller oaks where the green leaves have burst out of their buds, while the old brown leaves of last year are still attached to the branch. Can a tree come into leaf if it never lost its old leaves? It seems abnormal – an arboreal palimpsest, the oak rewriting itself, instead of completing the traditional cycle. On the way back there's a completely bare ash. It's one of my problems with folklore. I have the pedantic, particular streak of the naturalist. There's never enough detail in folklore. No references to chase up, no higher authorities to seek clarification from, as to whether it should be all ashes before all oaks, or does the first individual win it? Or does the oak that kept its old leaves invalidate the whole thing? Meanwhile the soil is pale and dusty and cracking up in the fields under the green layer of growing wheat. The rhyme 'April showers brings May flowers' persists in a dusty corner of my mind from childhood. I can't remember the last significantly wet April.

It is a Saturday as I write this. I have to check that – which day of the week, which day of which month. The pandemic has eroded my concept of time. Days merge and flow into weeks, while the numbers of global infections and global deaths keep rising, the only constant currently, like a sort of morbid measure of time. Global warming has altered the time and the order of spring. As oak is supposed to have overtaken ash, any almanac now would surely need to be a record of change, an almanac of uncertainty. But as the ash here beat the oak, it would need to be all specific instances, no generalisations, an appreciation that nothing is as it should be. I envy the almanacs their certainty of time.

I do find almanacs interesting and I am not alone. They are a naturalist's tendency in literary form. All the birdwatchers and naturalists I have spoken to agree about this – the passing and noticing of the seasons are important to us. When we left Dumfries I took my collection for enjoyment. In lockdown, almanacs seem as good a way as any to be transported out of my isolation. If I can't get out into nature this April beyond my immediate surroundings, then I can read Flora Thompson's *A Country Calendar* and briefly imagine being there, at her side, in 1920s Hampshire at 'primrose time . . . [when] every copse is a primrose copse, every path is a primrose path. One scent of the primrose is the very breath of April.'[10] And I am there, in an unexpected profusion of wild flowers that I'm more familiar with as garden plants that I sniff and get no scent from – maybe I just have a breathless April.

Thompson never published her calendar as such. It is comprised of uncollected writings for a niche journal, the *Catholic Fireside*, compiled by a later editor and biographer,

Margaret Lane. That feels an important part of its charm – it is fantastically unhurried. She writes as though what she is saying is phenomenally obvious, which gives her licence for an unexpected enthusiasm. Her enthusiasm takes in: memories of flowers, birdsong, hedgehogs and elm trees, and a curious custom where, in some parts of the country, the first butterfly of the year is regarded as a bringer of misfortune, to be chased, caught and killed. An 'early visitant' she writes – and now it's an unusual March if we haven't had regular butterflies by the end of the month. Even Gilbert White, also in Hampshire, saw his first butterflies in 1766 on 8 March: a brimstone and a small tortoiseshell, still the earliest species today.[11]

Thompson opens up the rhythms of nature, as she discerns its beat, from almost a century ago in a different end of the country, in a way that I can feel too. At times of worry, like now, it offers relief.

Last night I got lost.

On my allowed daily exercise, I walked to the local wood, seeing nobody as I went, and took a track I had never taken before. I wasn't sure if it was a path or not, for it had no markers and I had no map but the wood encouraged me. A giant white poplar guarded the entrance to the track in its shadowy, pale-edged way. It is a charismatic, beckoning tree, the siren sort that lures you in to look and then head further on. There was nobody around. Blackcap song floated through the trees. Blossom and leaf, bushes and tall trees. A muntjac disappeared through a brief blizzard of blossom, driven from the blackthorn by the breeze. Cowslips and primroses and their hybrid, the false oxlips, spangled the edge of the track with stars of lemon and butter. Leafwards, I slipped, into a green hypnosis.

I knew the direction the track was heading in and I knew the path that would intersect it, looping around to take me back. But as I walked, lost in the leaves, I didn't recognise it. I walked beyond. Guided by flowers – a cuckoo flower with its delicate lilac flower standing proud over the grass – and the encouragement of chiffchaff, blackcap and robin song. The track began to fade under my feet but I wasn't bothered: it was a lovely evening, enjoyment coursed through me, even though an obliterated pheasant – deconstructed into its feathers and viscera – lay in the grass. The sun was falling, the light failing; the wood started to feel as if it were closing in as the path thinned, the colours dimmed and the wrens disappeared into thick shadow. The sudden evening chill made me pull down the sleeves of my hoodie to my fingertips. The wood no longer enticing, I picked my pace up, keen to get back to the track that I knew, that I thought was ahead, when I turned a bend to see the end of the wood. The track reached a complete end in an impenetrable thicket, a pile of spent shotgun cartridges, and a barrage of signs nailed to the tree trunks: 'No Right of Way'; 'Shooting in Progress'. Shit.

I turned around. A kite skimmed the crown of the wood, turning its head, keeping an eye on me as it flew overhead. I retraced my steps, the wood now unfamiliar in reverse and what had seemed like a welcoming, beckoning walk was now becoming frantic. In the nature haze I had ignored the rutted ground under the grass, the trees felled over ditches that were clearly not safe walkways. When I'm alone, my imagination can run wild and I had the sense that any minute now I would come around a bend and find a man with a shotgun and no sense of humour. I kept seeing disorientating movements out of the corner of my eye. Wrens flicking through the undergrowth. White flash of muntjac scuts bursting through the pathside bushes. One buck eyeballed me down the path and stood its ground until I was five metres away, before running off with a clatter. Nothing felt real.

Half an hour after I left the path I knew, I refound the one I did. I walked it to where it met the main path through the wood and as I rejoined familiar ground, I noticed a sign I hadn't seen before: 'No Entry'.

This walk lives with me long after I get home, get warm again, get dinner. Over the next week I keep returning to it in my head, wondering. I don't understand why I didn't recognise the path. My memories don't fade, they already seem prefaded. As if I were drunk on nature, drunk on blossom, intoxicated by the green light that filters through the new leaves, which somehow lured me on, lured me out of my normal mind.

At the end of April it begins to rain, days of torrential downpours to make up for the rest of the month, to refill the ditches, turn the dusty soil to instant mud, slick and slippery, coating my trainers and jeans, filling the air with the rich and heady scent of spring. The word for it is petrichor but I don't need a word to know that smell of earth after rain is one of the finest things on earth. As we slip into May I come across a John Berger quote:

> It's the first week in May ... in the northern hemisphere, the leaves of most of the trees are coming out. Not only are all their different varieties of green still distinct, people also have the impression that each single leaf is distinct, and so they are confronting billions – no, not billions ... they are confronting an infinite multitude of new leaves.[12]

The world has been transformed by April, creating a riot of the senses: the feel of light on skin, the fragrance of rain on earth, of cut grass, the sight of chlorophyll coursing through the landscape and birdsong erupting from the hedgerows. The trees are leaved. The light still lengthens from here but only gradually now after all its early exuberance.

Egrets

It's wise not to make any rash predictions about birds. They have a tendency to prove you wrong.

A golden evening in early summer. There is a ditch that runs along the other side of the road, that channels the heavy rains away from the dry fields, a network of fake rivers for the flat landscape, giving water a place to run. Soon they will be dry here, or perhaps with the barest of trickles, a slight dampness from a wet spell or strong storm. But currently there is still water held within, even if I can't see it from my side of the road. Water holds promise. It holds potential and a little egret is circling over it, weighing it up. A startling presence here. It looks brilliant. Brilliant, from the French *briller*, meaning 'sparkling', for they always seem to absorb and reflect light, as if each egret has spent every second of the day being polished to bright perfection under the brilliant sunlight. It turns away on its slow wings – not this ditch, not this day – slowly beating its way towards the River Ivel, a few miles from here.

And it reminds me of one of my more rash predictions. Just before we moved to Dumfries I pointed out some little egrets to Miranda, and I stupidly suggested they might be the last we saw for a while. The first time we got out to the Solway Firth we saw a flock of ten. A few trips later we saw the great white egret – an even bigger surprise – hunting in the saltmarsh channels. I was out of date. Miles off. They had progressed while I continued to believe they petered out towards the border. Birds have a tendency to be self-willed. Egrets especially.

We keep secrets under blue skies when a new species breeds for the first time. We keep them all season, until the breeders have departed on autumn migration. Bird eggs are still a sought-after commodity for a rump of recidivists who have an addiction to raiding nests and taking entire eggs, drilling a little hole to extract the yolk, and then keeping the shell in a secret, illegal collection. Rarity has a value and the eggs of the newest species to breed in a place are the most valuable of all. It happened in 1996: in two places on the south coast of England, two precious little egret nests. One in the heronry of Brownsea Island in Dorset, the other, at a mainland site, has been kept secret. This wasn't entirely unexpected. Wandering little egrets had been incredibly rare in Britain until 1989, an irruptive year when a flock of forty arrived, sparking thoughts that perhaps they might 'temporarily' extend their breeding range here.[1]

I like the word 'temporarily' in this context. As if it was still difficult to comprehend, even then, that this delicate bird – of slender build and splendid feathers – might settle properly, here at the northern fringe of its range; that Sussex would suffice instead of the great southern European wetlands. Perhaps it would be tempting fate: sod's law, or the punishment of the fickle gods of birding to be overconfident, to wish for more.

We got more. Now secrecy is lax: the wetlands of England, Wales and Ireland are studded with glistening white herons. It would take something more than a disaster to reverse this now.

The pattern repeated, with variations. As well as little and great white egret, the other species we have in Europe is the cattle egret; as well as little and large cattle egret, we have a stocky egret, more at home in cattle fields, with a stubby orange bill for catching what the cows disturb.

In 2008 the cattle egret first bred in England, in Somerset, after a large influx that was reminiscent of how the little egret colonised. Expectations had changed. The Rare Breeding Birds Panel report for 2008 suggests 'it may be that this species is here to stay'.[2] But then a few fallow years: years without attempts, before the great white egret stole their thunder in 2012, also breeding in Somerset, and managing to stay there consistently, breeding every year. By 2016 they had managed to break out from Somerset (a sort of heaven for herons) and breed in Norfolk too. Great white seems to have found colonising much smoother than cattle egret. Cattle egret managed three nests in three English counties in 2019: the website BirdGuides drily described this at the time as 'the species' seemingly inevitable – but drawn out – colonisation'.[3] It is a rare thing – a special thing indeed – to see wild animals of any description making such geography-defying movements, to set up new populations, new outposts in new parts of the world, a rare example of good news, in this warming world.

I became blasé about the great white egret on the Solway, seeing it so regularly, in a flat brown-green landscape where anything heron-sized and bright white would stand out, despite it feeling like a miracle that it survived the storm. I have to remind myself with every little egret that I see that, as a British breeding bird, this species is younger than me; its presence here is an irruptive miracle in a time of mass declines, a simple symbol of hope and avian survival. Especially in the way that circling over ditches in the golden evening light, by the dry fields of Bedfordshire, has become normal.

Later, I learn that this summer was the one: that Scotland's first breeding pair of little egrets had spent the summer raising young on the Solway, somewhere (note the deliberately imprecise location) in Dumfries and Galloway, while I was marooned in Bedfordshire.[4] A new toehold in a new country, the march of the egrets continuing.

3

Fractured Rhythms

Google Street View plunges me into the wrong season. It's the difference two months makes: the images were taken in March 2009, evidently a cold, late year, and the grass is dull green, and everything else is tarnished with the rust of late winter. The sky is white and cold and I do an involuntary shiver as I drive my laptop screen down the single-track road, past bare birches and mossy oaks. I miss the innocence of last winter when we were free, but having tasted the warmth of early summer, it's not what I need now. J. A. Baker, cycling down an Essex country lane, 'swooped through leicestershires of swift green light',[1] while with each click I stutter through the fixed pixels of a long-dead winter, nothing swift, nothing light.

I am sitting in my bedroom, alone, travelling virtually: a side effect of this year's disorientations, the year where everything is wrong. The disconnect between the world outside the window and the one on my screen is striking. It makes me feel seasonally disorientated, searching for summer in a place where it is absent. There is a science to this. Phenology is the study of events in life cycles; the first frog spawn, the average bird-egg laying date or last sighting of a butterfly species, for example. Phenology is measured against time and climate; it's a way of tracking what's happening and why.

Phenological mismatch is what happens when this begins to go wrong, when the seasonal events that were in order begin to warp and overtake one another. And what happens to the wildlife as their natural rhythms fall apart.

It is to the Wood of Cree I am virtually driving. I have never been to the Wood of Cree. I still haven't, though I'm trying, in the absence of anywhere else to go. I'm trying still to be a naturalist, to experience summer, even if there are no summer birds to see on my digital tour.

Wood of Cree specialises in three species, the ones that I really cherish the chance to see in summer. It is a rare wood but a good wood that holds all three: the common redstart, the pied flycatcher and the wood warbler.

You'll find all three at the same end of your field guide. Field guides are classically arranged in an evolutionary order, the birds placed by biological relationship rather than anything more practical. Redstarts and flycatchers are members of the Muscicapoidea (which means 'flycatcher'), a family of essentially robin-like birds. The wood warbler comes a section after them, a member of the Sylvioidea, like the blackcap and chiffchaff, but where those two warblers are sufficiently robust to be garden species, the wood warbler, along with the redstart and the pied flycatcher, is a bit more specialist.

These three are linked not by the aeons of evolution, but by the whim of preference. They all have a liking for woodlands on the western edge of Britain, a fondness for the oaks and insects of the rolling hills and valleys of the wetter side of the country. All three species are long-distance migrants, choosing every summer to return to these trees from West Africa. The joy, the genius, and the trouble of migratory birds: they connect us with every square inch, every country, wood, thicket, sea and city between Scotland and Ghana, Guinea and Senegal. Together they are the most attractive and charismatic species of summer woodlands. Together they are all being absolutely hammered by what's happening to the world.

My new methodology for the locked-down naturalist: Google Street View, Google Earth, Ordnance Survey maps and management plans.

I find my digital drive to the Wood of Cree instructive. I cross up and out of town, beside empty fields and past empty blocks of conifer plantations. It's fine. Scenic but not particularly interesting until the road drops down again, where it cleaves to the course of the River Cree and the woods become deciduous, old and wild all the way through to the end of the road. The Wood of Cree is the largest ancient woodland in the south of Scotland, and it is, unusually, getting bigger. The RSPB, which manages a reserve here, recently planted 200,000 native trees because even ancient woodlands need to keep an eye on the future.[2]

I park my digital car. I switch to Google Earth, which reveals this part of Galloway to be just varying shades of green and brown, trees and moor, the contours smoothed out by the perspective. It's when I turn to the OS map – more real than the real thing – that the surroundings begin to make sense. It differentiates between the conifer and the deciduous; it marks out the texture of the ground, distinguishes the river from the shadows of trees. Just east of the wood, the map marks five cairns, a chambered cairn, a stone circle and the standing stones known as 'the thieves'. It's an ancient landscape here between the hills, rivers and trees, and I wonder if our ancestors felt that same sublime rush of leaf-light, the chlorophyllia of trees gorging on sunshine, as I do when I enter a good old wood on a sunny morning, or if that would have been so common as to be completely unremarkable.

I turn to a conservation report. Under the acronym bingo* of a place like this, the picture is that the wood is wet. Really wet. Wet enough to be thought of as temperate rainforest, while the lacework of burns that runs down from the high hills to the east frequently floods. When they do, they swallow the fields I drove past on Google Maps, the picnic benches, the car park and most of the road to the reserve as well. This wetness makes the wood a productive place for insects to hatch, which fuels an incredibly good breeding ground for birds.

Within the ground cover of blaeberry (the delicious deciduous shrub), bluebells and burnet-saxifrage, up to

---

* Wood of Cree is an NNR, SSSI, SAC, SRDP, SAM, a RAMSAR, UKBAP site (six times) and a UKHAP site. This is the full-house method of saying it's quite special.

eighteen pairs of wood warblers will be attempting to nest about now. High up in the canopy the pied flycatchers will be singing. At the forest edges, redstarts will be flitting out of the shade, flaring red flashes in the sunlight.

This collection of song and flora is historic. It was somewhere along the Cree that Robert Burns, listening intently for the voice of his lover, is briefly mistaken by 'the balmy breathing gale, / Mixt with some warbler's dying fall'. I wonder if this was a wood warbler (I suspect it was more likely the melancholy song of a willow warbler). The point of the poem is not the bird but Burns's lover and his desire to 'let us all our vows renew, / Along the flowery banks of the Cree'.[3]

I feel this keenly. My virtual tour is enjoyable but has left me with a deeper longing for where I should have been this year, among the sessile oak and blaeberry; the birds that I know and the plants that I don't. I end with a renewed vow that when this is all over I will visit it properly. I can imagine all the constituent parts, apply them to the contours of the map and the paths that wrinkle through the wood. But it's lacking something – that essence, the hard-to-define frisson of excitement that comes from first-hand experience, lost to the lockdown. After all, 'the living bird', as Margaret Atwood wrote, 'is not its labelled bones'.[4]

I still remember my first encounters with my summer woodland trinity. When I was younger, I had a ruse going with my parents during exam season. I would insist on being driven across the country for the prolonged period of distraction-free reading I could do in the car. My parents thought this was a good idea for my academic achievement. I thought it was a brilliant excuse to see birds. I remember Iggy Pop blaring on the stereo of Dad's old black Ford Mondeo as we came up through Staffordshire on the A523 and dropped down into one of the wooded ventricles of England's old rolling green heart. The Coombes Valley.

Lust for life indeed. I remember it vividly. Old and wet and rolling up the sides of a valley, innumerable shades of green and the hypnotic sequin shimmer of oak leaves in the gentle breeze. The effort that should have gone into revising for my AS Level ICT exam went into revising my three target species instead (I failed the exam so badly I wasn't even given a grade for it).

The flycatcher and the warbler were new for me. I had studied their unfamiliar songs: double-checked their unfamiliar plumages, looked at maps of the wood and where they were likely to be found. But none of this prepared me for the vivid verdancy of it. I wasn't aware things could be this green. This was, I felt then, the spirit of summer woodland.*

A few minutes down the path, I heard a sound I didn't recognise. I traced the trees with my binoculars, my vision all green sessile oak leaves, brown twigs and a sudden flash of red. Redstart! It is similar in size to a robin but the shape is sleeker, slightly elongated. The adult male has a plumage that, from the tip of its tail to just under its throat, is a vivid

---

* I was seventeen. Old enough to make a sweeping generalisation, young enough to do it earnestly.

red. Its throat and face are a glossy black, radiating to an ash-grey back, with just a startling white line on the forehead. It could have been designed. The fashionista's robin.

Its elegance goes beyond looks. As it perched on that oak branch, it turned its grey back to me. Its fire tail flickered. It is a thing definitive of the entire redstart family:* 'start' comes from old English *steort* for 'tail'. But it's also modern English for a sudden involuntary movement and that seems right too – the red tail shivers and seems to move of its own accord, trembling more like an autumn leaf in the breeze than a bird.

Some thrills are diminished by the expectation of them. But I've never found that with birds. I rounded the corner. Something shot through the corner of my vision. And again. I caught it fully at the third attempt. An unusual boomeranging motion: a bird somersaulting off its perch and returning to where it began. Flycatching. My first pied flycatcher, a male: glistening white underneath, velvet-black-backed and a large flash of white in the shivering wings that launched him after the flies.

The male flitted from his perch, deeper into the oak. Behind him, a female: the same grey-brown shade of tree bark, a more delicate tracery of white around her wing feathers. By the end of the summer, he will have moulted his black-and-white plumage into something like her grey-brown. The genus they belong to – the Ficedula – has an

---

* There are fifteen true redstart species across the old world. Only two occur in Britain, the common redstart I am describing here and the black redstart, a species of the urban fringe.

intriguing etymology. The word is translated into Latin out of the Greek for 'fig-eater'. It was also used for the blackcap by Aristotle and medieval naturalists. Whether it was merely a misidentification or they were thought to transform into the blackcap in autumn, we'll never know. Although moult is as much a transformation as anything else. The avian equivalent of the turning tree leaves.

As a teenager I had little confidence in anything other than my ability to find birds. At Coombes Valley this ornithological conviction was to be tarnished. Dad and I came here, rather than any closer wood, for the certainty that there were wood warblers, the hardest of the three species to find, the one most restricted to the west. We walked every trail. We listened to every song, scoured the canopy with our binoculars, saw many flaring redstarts and somersaulting pied flycatchers, but could not, for all our desperate searching, find any trace of the wood warbler.

I didn't see one until a year later, on another bright May morning. Reading *Hamlet* on the M6 – the ruse still working – we were heading west of the West Midlands to the Wyre Forest of Worcestershire, early R.E.M. on the stereo of Dad's new silver Mondeo. Where Coombes Valley was a riot of life, the Wyre was more manicured and ordered and neater. The path from the car park runs along a disused railway line, halfway up the side of the valley, and though the experience of the wood is less luxuriously wild for it, the ease with which you pass from the human world to the world of ancient woodland is wonderful. This is assisted by the wood warbler. We heard our first just out of the car park. As we walked down the old railway track, towering oaks on both sides, wood-warbler song clattered from the canopy. We scanned intensely, searching for the leaf-green warbler with a face of lemon yellow, breast of pure white, lurking in the leaves. It stopped singing. And after a few beats, a few fruitless scans, it dropped down from the canopy to the lower branches of the tree. I had forgotten that though they sing in the canopy, they nest on the ground, going up and down like an avian yo-yo.

There are three things that all the research I had done into finding a wood warbler did not prepare me for. I knew it was green and yellow and white, but I hadn't expected the vibrancy of it – the effervescence of its lemon-painted face or the grass-green fringes to the wing feathers, and how they stood out from its white underparts. I had not been aware of the size of it, like a willow warbler on steroids, with long wings hanging off a plump, teardrop-shaped body. And the volume of its song: I knew what it sounded like, that it was no feeble warble, but I was amazed by the gusto with which it was delivered, as the bird sat sideways across a branch, its body tilted back, singing with such body-shaking force that even its wings trembled with the effort. It is often likened to a coin spinning – a short, sharp clatter, a crescendo until the coin falls. But it's delivered with the intense spinning energy of a Catherine wheel. It was perfect.*

* I was eighteen at this point and the irony and coolness with which I greeted the world extended to everything but birds. About birds I was still absolutely, sickeningly earnest.

And though that day in the Wyre I would see many brilliant things – it was one of those rare birding days when all that is good and difficult and unusual seems to flaunt itself in front of your binoculars – it's still the barely-holding-its-feathers-together wood-warbler song that stands out above everything else that day.

My memory works well for wildlife I've seen. It's shoddy on everything else. So my new methodology for the locked-down naturalist falters somewhat with phenological mismatch. I can't remember when I first heard about it, when I first learned of this elegantly simple, subtly malign cause behind much of our wildlife declines; when it first began to sink in that what we've done to the planet has had such a thorough reach in destabilising everything. I wish I could isolate what I felt then and extrapolate it, to pull out a productive feeling or emotion from the dawning horror. But it's been lost to some dusty corner in my mind, filed away with the rest of the gloomy environmental forecasts.

Phenology is the progression of the season, the synchronised order by which one event allows another to happen. Phenological mismatch is when that goes wrong, when things get knocked off course. It is the real sting in the tail with nature: the way that effects knock into each other and compound themselves; ecology becoming an unexpected game of dominoes.

Between Guinea-Bissau in Africa and Nant Brân woods in Wales lies almost three thousand miles of inhospitable terrain: sea, desert, mountain; the cities of Casablanca, Lisbon and Cardiff. Pied flycatchers must cross it twice a year on their migration: small feathers, fuelled by insects. It is one of the many unsung miracles of nature that this is possible, and it is heartening that it still happens roughly as it was supposed to. But these birds are being stung by the competing demands of ecology. Every year this distance does not change; it is a fixed fact of life, like the length of a day. The same cannot be said of other factors that affect the pied flycatcher's phenology.

It is general ornithological theory – the phenological match – that you lay your eggs before your food supply is at its most abundant. You synchronise, so that when you have five to seven hungry chicks chirping at you from the shadow of your nest in a rotting tree hole, you have ample prey to catch and regurgitate into the maws of your blind and naked young. Your prey are caterpillars and the oak woodlands you migrate to should be stuffed full of them.

Caterpillar populations are measurable by frass, the fabulously specific word for caterpillar shit. Frass looks, I'm told, a lot like instant coffee granules that fall as a gentle, mostly unnoticed rain from the treetops at the height of the breeding season. Mostly unnoticed: scientists have ways of registering this, because it is important. The peak of frass is the time of peak caterpillar availability. But when that happens is changing. Every year Dr Rob Thomas of Cardiff University tracks the progression of spring by measuring the lengths of oak leaves from across the country. The point of this is to work out how their growth varies; spring coming early means better, bigger leaves. The caterpillars respond to the leaves that respond to the climate.

Blue tits and great tits are resident in the woods and usually tailor their timings to the caterpillars. The great tit lays its eggs so that its peak demand for caterpillars to feed its chicks falls, on average, two days after the date of peak caterpillar availability in the woods (it is three days for the blue tit).[5] But one study found that if the date of peak caterpillar availability sped up by ten days, the blue and great tits were able to advance their egg-laying only by five days from the average.

It is even harder for the pied flycatchers – they managed just three days. They must still cross that fixed distance of three thousand miles. By looking at data from North Ronaldsay Bird Observatory, it was discovered that pied flycatchers are migrating in spring 1.4 days earlier every year.[6] This, however, is not enough to keep up. Their peak demand for caterpillars has fallen twelve days behind the peak availability. In one studied year, when it was warm and the leaves came early, they had fallen twenty-seven days behind peak caterpillar.[7] Of the phenological misfits, the pied flycatcher seems to be one of the most affected; they are dropping out of sync with a summer that arrives too early for them.*

Dr Rob Thomas has a passion for pied flycatchers. On a quiet summer's day in the wood of Nant Brân, in Powys,

---

* This year has been an exceptionally warm April and May, an early spring. I am worried for them.

bathed in the green light of sunshine and oak, he found an urgent scene. An abandoned pied flycatcher nest: five of the six chicks dead and the survivor covered in their shit. There was only one thing to do. He took it home. His young daughter has a knack for looking after animals and they cleaned it up, fed it mealworms and any caterpillars he could find. He named it Mayfly, optimistically.

'After a few days,' he told me,

> she became quite tame, and would fly around the room and land on people's heads and shoulders. I took her to a school lesson or two, to teach the kids about birds and woodlands and migration. At that time I was growing some oak saplings in my office at university, so Mayfly used to come with me in a cage and then fly around my office and sit in the oak trees. It looked very authentic. When she was fully fledged, we ringed and released her back into the same woodland. She flew up into the canopy and quickly began feeding for herself. A week or so later, I was sitting in the wood (marking some exam essays!) and a ringed juvenile pied flycatcher came very close and sat looking at me for a while: I'd like to think that was Mayfly.

In the current state of affairs, every pied flycatcher matters. Conservation is going to struggle to stem the tide of phenological mismatch: endeavours like Mayfly are inevitably last-ditch, the aversion of a small disaster that just might, in the long run, contribute to the aversion of a bigger one.

My summer trinity is vanishing. Redstart is on the amber list of conservation concern, while the wood warbler has joined the pied flycatcher on the red list.

Looking through the British Trust for Ornithology's *Atlas of British Birds* projects, the steady decline of the wood warbler is clear to see. The first atlas, comprising four years of surveying from 1968 to 1972, reveals a good scattering of red dots – each one an area with breeding wood warblers – across the country, the main area of absence being from eastern England, from Essex through to North Yorkshire. I toggle to the map from the second atlas, this time from 1988 to 1991. The Midlands and the southeast of England suffer a swingeing hit. Red dots disappear into white nothing. Devon and Hampshire remain as strongholds in the south. Wales remains densely populated with them and a strong population runs like a spine north from the Peak District to the Scottish Highlands. The last atlas map, from 2007 to 2011, is where the trauma lies. In Hampshire they are restricted to the New Forest. The Devon population is split in two, north and south. That spine up the country is now riddled with holes and, as I found at Coombes Valley, any attempt to see them now risks being a year too late: the spring the wood warblers stopped coming.

Wales and the west coast of Scotland remain as strong-holds. But I can toggle to another map. The 'breeding abundance change' is another, more accurate way of view-ing things. It is an alternative distribution map, one in which the populations are coloured in a spectrum of shades of red, white and blue. Dark red for increasing, white for no change and dark blue for decreasing. And the Welsh and Scottish strongholds are all the darkest shade of blue. There are no red squares in all of Wales and only three light red squares in England. For most of the country, the penny drop at the end of their spinning-coin song will not be picked up again, and spring will be a more silent, less perfect, less tender time.

The worst part is that we don't really know why. Phenological mismatch does not explain this – their diet is wide enough to incorporate the full spectrum of insects; they don't need to catch the wave of caterpillars like others do. They don't return to the same nesting areas after each spring migration. They defy the logic of their kind. They are not doing as badly elsewhere in Europe, only here where our summer is reduced to 6,500 singing males, as if they are retreating from the northwestern edge of their range. Conservation is an ongoing project, an almost forensic piecing together of minute details. Work is frantically being done between the glens of the Highlands and the forests of Ghana, investigating the insects, the habitats, the climate. And all that it has unearthed so far is more questions, while the warbler seems more spirit-like, harder to grasp, as impossible to pin down as they are in the woodland canopy. The absence of an obvious smoking gun is deeply worrying.

There is a selfishness at the heart of my sadness here. Birding is my mental and physical refuge from whatever else is happening. It levels my moods out, keeps me feeling sane and gives me great joy when I have one of those semi-regular encounters with a wild animal that leaves me thrilled and reminded of my place in the world. The decline of birds diminishes this. When I saw my first wood warbler I could talk about it only in sentences of hyphenated breathlessness. Each lost bird rebounds back onto me; one less chance to feel the truth of Wendell Berry's poem, 'The Peace of Wild Things'.[8]

Phenology is not just a spring and summer phenomenon; as we've already seen, what happens in winter directly affects what happens in other seasons. But neither is it something restricted to what is happening in the UK.

The Sahel in Africa is an incredibly important area for birds. An arid but fertile area south of the Sahara, between the desert and the savannah, it is the first safe land after the desert-crossing when heading south, and the last safe land on the return journey.

But that safe land is unpredictable. The Sahel is even more prone to the turbulence of an unsettled climate than other parts of the planet. The droughts are long and harsh and deadly: it is estimated that 100,000 people died in the drought between the 1960s and 1980s,[9] others argue that it never ended and that the last fifty years have been one long drought.[10]

We live on a shared planet and a tragedy like this for humans impacts on birds too. European bird populations are inextricably linked with the rainfall of the Sahel, even though they never see it. The wet season ends in October, and begins again in spring, after they have returned north. During that period of drought, declines were recorded in several European birds that spend the winter in the Sahel;

the common example is the whitethroat, a small *Sylvia* warbler, that in the summer of 1969 was found to have declined by 77 per cent on the year before.[11] Many European birds are reliant on rain in Africa.

A Dutch book, *Living on the Edge*, scores species based on the importance of the Sahel to them, on a scale from 1 to 7, with 7 being strongly dependent on the Sahel. The wood warbler and pied flycatcher score a 4, for they predominantly spend the winter further south. The Sahel is still essential for them, though, as they pause there before continuing their journey. In drought years, the Sahel is no longer a temporary refuge, a stepping stone during migration for tired birds from the desert; it is the desert.

Redstarts, however, score a 7; they spend the winter in the Sahel, in the places where there are still trees. What rain falls is enough to kindle acacia trees into flower, harbouring insects for the redstarts to eat. These summer rains in the Sahel are a vital part of a redstart's phenology, one that tends to be obscured by British-centric data, where redstarts have sustained a relatively consistent level of population despite the drought-induced declines elsewhere.* *Living on the Edge* points out that in Sweden, Switzerland and the Netherlands '[Redstarts] crashed in the late 1960s and early 1970s and have remained at consistently low levels since.'[12] You can map out the rises in their population with the years of good

* It is thought that the redstarts from mainland Europe winter in drier, more central parts of the Sahel, and so were affected more than the British birds.

rain. Our summer woodland depends on the winter in the Sahel.

There's a more general point at play here: that two of the sharpest and apparently most intractably declining groups of British birds are our woodland birds and our migratory birds. My trio falls under both these brackets. It's hard to escape the sense that nature is stressed, that the systems that support our life are stretching, fraying; that there is less food and less space for the birds that are still flying the same distance every year. It's no wonder that something gives out. Surveys have shown that the species doing well are the generalists and the short-distance migrants. The less highly strung, the less dependent on things being as they expect. It seems as though our woods, our world, as well as becoming more silent, are becoming plainer, less interesting, less able to provide a home to the niche species.

Recovery is a slower act than loss. We are running out of time for the redstart across Europe, for the pied flycatcher and the wood warbler here in Britain; for all three in the Sahel and sub-Saharan Africa. Our migratory birds remind us that our world is connected, that 'no island is an island', if you will. What affects and troubles us in Britain affects and troubles everyone everywhere. Phenology extends beyond a single season, area and habitat: the potential for mismatch grows bigger as the seasons warp and destabilise.

Each wood is not one thing but as Whitman said, they 'contain multitudes'.[13] And we are losing the multitudes, the myriad and the many from our woods. The glittering green of our summer woodlands changes over the course of the season, dulling, the tannins growing stronger in the leaves, the chlorophyll gorged on sunlight from its natural, naked colour in spring, before the leaf develops other pigments and grows thicker, waxier. The longer the season goes on, the darker the woodlands get. It seems to me that losing the exuberance of my trinity of birds would be like skipping that bright, light-green stage.

If we lose all three, we will lose them in increments, one by one, like stars slowly disappearing in the early-morning sky. Then summer won't be the same. It'll be like my virtual Wood of Cree made real. I'll finally be standing in the actual wood, able only to imagine all the lost species that are no longer bringing the woodlands alive; piecing together the birds from their bones, the place from the memories of what once was.

Dragonflies

I offer him my index finger. He takes it, slowly, clambering up from the scalding tarmac of the road, one pair of legs at a time. The sensation is like having a spider crawl over my hand, the tickle of his leg bristles, the sure grip of the claw-like point of his foot, the surprise of his weightless body.

Dragonflies look perfect, almost mechanical. This one is an emperor, a particularly robust example of the order, which is what prompted me to bend down and make my offer. You don't normally find emperors on country roads.

In my hand, I can see the problem. His neck is broken. His head is wrenched around at 180 degrees: the guillotine of his jaws on top, eyes under. It takes a second for the ghastliness of it to sink in, while my mind scrabbles for reasons. Hit by a car, I guess, but only a glancing blow. A fatal wound and a long-drawn-out death to come.

In my hand he is alive, one glorious last time. I am torn between the horror of the injury and the beauty of his body. The thorax, apple bright, adjoining an abdomen made of segments of brilliant, kingfisher blue.* A thick black line runs down

---

* The abdomen is green in the female.

the abdomen with spurs, like painted vertebrae. It's the wings that really catch my eye. Normally they are a blur. Now their delicacy and strength are apparent. Thin black veins trace a honeycomb-like pattern through the transparent membrane, with a milky-tea-coloured pane – the pterostigma – towards the tip. The hind wings are shorter but deeper, the inside edge curving towards the abdomen, where a narrow segment accommodates this kink. The leading edge of the forewing – the costa – is a pale lemon yellow. Then I'm back at the apple thorax, noticing a slight, light downiness. And the problem – his perfect head, broken.

I take the coward's way out. I can't kill him. I transfer him to a branch in the hedge, and hope nature takes its course.

A few days later I return. These sunny days feel like a broadcast in high definition. The ring of trees and gently folded hills shine through the still air that holds them without haze. The road is quiet. And when I get back to the branch in the hedge, I find him in the grass beneath. His head gone, the thorax opened up and hollowed out, the faded abdomen a brittle shell, as thin as a cigarette paper.

Tennyson saw in a dragonfly 'a living flash of light'.[1] For the poet, priest and profound enthusiast for nature, Gerard Manley Hopkins, 'dragonflies draw flame'.[2] Yet this extinguished emperor stays in my mind, long after its slowly dimmed abdomen fades away. The first sentence in my field guide is that 'Dragonflies are the essence of summer,'[3] and there is some truth to what the poets are getting at: the intensity and brightness of them, inherent to the season. The fire of the sun and the flash of light that falls between shadows. Their obvious size and bold behaviour, not slipping barely seen along the vegetated edges of a watercourse as damselflies do.

I saw one in the forest, last summer, paused on a metal gate. Its long, thin abdomen dangling down from its perch; paired spots of sky blue on black, yellow notches at the join of each segment. It clung to the sun-warmed metal, long wings outstretched. On the thorax, thin green antehumeral stripes, green face, big blue eyes. A common hawker, perched like a crucifix.

It leapt into action, buzzing, skimming the treeline, cutting across the path, exploring the other side, turning on a point, its hawking flight its defining feature; a burst of energy in the lethargic doldrums of a long summer afternoon.

Time passed quickly, absorbed as we were in the zipping energy of the only thing flying in the sultry hours. And the claim that dragonflies are the essence of summer felt a little more like a factual statement, as the hawker slipped through the thick forest shadows to fluoresce in a shock of sunlight.

4

Living Landscapes

I don't dream much. But I have found lapwings in my nights these past few weeks. The breeding season is at its height and I am back at North Ronaldsay, down the entrance track from the bird observatory, by the marsh at the back of Loch Gretchen. It's where the lapwings breed, where I used to pause every sunny day and watch them. Their display flights are the joy of the season distilled. Each one turns into a stunt pilot: swooping up, then diving, barrel-rolling because they can, because their wings are short and broad, designed for agility and short bursts of speed. It gives them a level of control that lets them turn daredevil. As they carve up the sky, they call out – making electric sounds, unearthly whoops of joy, onomatopoeic of their old country names, 'peewit' and 'pyewipe'. But then birds are not of the earth but the air: lighter and brighter. As the lapwings spiral, their plumage flashes iridescent green and purple in the summer sun, jewel-like – the green of the grass, the purple of marsh orchids, the colours of a summer marsh made avian.

I have always known lapwings like this: as specialists of marshlands, somewhere between water and grass, sky and mud, best seen from RSPB hides. But it wasn't always this way: they were once a grassland and farmland bird, common across the wider landscape, before successive changes to agriculture cleared them away from our fields, isolating them on the tiny percentage of land that comprises our wetland nature reserves.

What this means is that losses get reinforced. Without the memory of what was once present, without the 'normal' as a baseline, each loss becomes internalised to the next generation as the 'normal'. There is a slow erosion of life this way: what is normal, what we expect, gets progressively less diverse, less interesting. Ecologists call this 'shifting baseline syndrome'. Think of it as a sort of red shift: the irresistible movement of all that is of interest towards the red list of conservation concern. Or, in the ghastly phrase of now, the 'new normal'.

The world changes for us and them. We both adapt. And now I think that there's nothing unusual in needing to go to a nature reserve to see a lapwing.

Charles St John, a nineteenth-century naturalist and hunter living in the Scottish Highlands, left us a valuable if little-read record of its birds. In the short foreword to my edition, Robert Dougall, the broadcaster and one-time RSPB president writes, 'There seemed to be birds every-where':[1] a poignant record of a lost time of avian abundance. When St John walks the fields near him at night, 'I hear the peewits rising near me.'[2] Lapwings were then common enough to provide regular observation, not just of their daily habits but of their nests: their breeding ('nidification', he says) was common enough to be unexceptional, to experiment with.

St John's interactions with his nidifying lapwings went so far as to include picking the young up before they can fly, to watch the parents' reaction. The adults head straight for him, 'as if about to fly in your face.'[3] While nowadays this would be hugely discouraged – obviously, the lapwing is a rare bird and it would be unacceptable to disturb their nests while the young are vulnerable – a part of me lingers over this with regret. That rarity also precludes the chance to experience a field education like this: hands-on and experimental, the sort of encounter that real lessons are learned from. Populations are not the only things that can be lost when species decline.

Now the modern lapwing lives in places such as Mersehead, my local RSPB reserve in Dumfries and Galloway. Last winter I was fortunate enough to be shown around the reserve by the RSPB's area manager, Andrew Bielinski, and a revolving cast of the reserve's staff members. It was a dry December's day, before it rained for the rest of the winter, and the marsh was green, more grass than water. Bielinski and his staff were rewetting it for my mind's eye, explaining the specific needs of the lapwings and redshanks that they were hoping to attract to breed. Waders, they explained, had become the conservation priority for the area.

Sometimes you need to believe the numbers over your eyes. We sat watching a long string of lapwings flying back and forth restlessly over the marsh, as if their eyes in the air had clocked a danger that was not apparent to us, earthbound and enclosed in an old, cold, wooden hide. The action of their broad wings is not exactly laboured, in the sense that they don't seem to be struggling to do it, but measured in the sense that each wingbeat looks deliberate. They banked away from us, their emerald backs briefly blending in with the conifer-clad hillside that forms the northeast horizon. Then side-on as they flew back across, flashing light and dark with each wingbeat. Eventually they settled down and through my telescope I could make out the purple gloss to the emerald back. A light ginger fringe to some of the feathers of the younger birds. Their white face has a crucifix of dark lines meeting over the eye, the vertical line becoming a dark cap on top of their head. Over the nape it comes together in a few fine feathers curling up and away from the head. I think it's important to note when nature looks ridiculous. The crest of a lapwing looks ridiculous – like the extravagantly curling feathers of a formal military parade cap.

There are two types of marsh here, fresh marsh and saltmarsh. Saltmarsh forms in low-energy areas. In the context of the Solway Firth, Southwick Water is one such place, a small river that threads its way behind the Mersehead fresh marsh, before unravelling into small hill burns. It exploits a little dent in the coastline, a gap between the sand dunes that run between the fresh marsh and the firth, and the rest of the rockier coastline west of the reserve. It opens up a triangle of merse, the local term for saltmarsh. Merse is where the debate between water and land reaches its extremes. The tide takes over the land with water, then the tide gives it back. The tide and the flow of the river carve the land into intricate patterns. The salt in the seawater restricts the vegetation that coats the land to what is just hardy enough to survive. The mud in the creeks is exceptionally rich in unseen energy, invertebrates including the mud shrimps and molluscs that lurk just beneath the surface. I've often heard people compare the calories in a cubic metre of estuary mud to a number of Mars bars (normally either fourteen or sixteen – I have been unable to trace it back to a reputable source). The mud here in this saltmarsh is estuary mud on a tiny scale before it flows into the firth, an estuary on a massive scale.

Saltmarsh is great for waders. They flow with the tides: onto the mud at low tide, onto the land at high. Fresh marsh is often more static, a more predictable environment (unless it really rains), whereas merse is wild and alive. As are the birds. Which have all, this day, chosen to be on the fresh marsh.

We are not short of lapwings to look at. This is true of most British wetlands in winter, when lapwings from Central and Eastern Europe populations migrate westwards for our milder winters, forming a winter population of 620,000.[4] In summer it is a different story. Lapwings are site-faithful birds: they return to nest in the same fields in successive summers. When the winter birds return to mainland Europe, we are left with those that breed here, roughly 96,500 pairs.[5] This number sounds good, not rare at all, until you realise this is another shifting baseline: that number is down by 80 per cent from the 1960s, a third down in the last twenty years.[6] Farmland comprises the habitat for 95 per cent of our breeding lapwings,[7] but their needs are not compatible with the march for efficiency. They prefer a mix of arable and cattle farming: crops to nest in, pasture to feed in. But those crops need to be sown in spring: crops sown in autumn grow too long too soon in the year for lapwings to nest in, their habitat outgrowing them while they sit tight to the soil, swamped in green. Hot summers, where the landscape is parched, are also detrimental to them, perhaps explaining their flight from the farmlands to the wetlands.

I don't blame farmers for this. It is a hard life and commercial logic is compelling: the metric you are measured by is your yield of wheat, not waders. But the outlook for lapwings, as we once knew them, appears bleak. And this is why managing Mersehead and other wetlands for waders is so important: their future here seems to depend entirely on how well the majority of them makes the switch to reserves from the traditional farmland.

A wetland might be defined by its water but the land is important too. Mud and grasses. What is not helpful, if your conservation priority is attracting amber- and red-listed waders to your marsh, is that they all like different configurations of water, mud and grass. For lapwings: short, grazed grass and shallow water. For redshanks: damp soil is a minimum, shallow water good; short grass is needed for feeding, tall grass for nesting. For curlew: tall vegetation, rough, tussocky ground, only lightly grazed. For snipe: extensively graze your wet grassland but not in the breeding season. For oystercatchers: any flat, hard surface will suffice.

They nest on a roundabout on the A75 at Castle Douglas; they called all night long from the roof of my student halls of residence – which is not what you expect of a species that is vulnerable across Europe. Waders are like Goldilocks. Or perhaps it's better to say that each marsh is a Rubik's cube of cows, grass, water and mud, that solving it for one side ruins it for another. There is no general, all-purpose marsh for a wader.

It is uplifting seeing the lapwings in winter. It is a good grounding in what the past must have looked like and how the future could look if we solve the puzzle, if our conservation efforts pay out in glittering green ribbons of lapwing in the sky. But it is early summer now: the time to be in a wetland, when the breeding season is reaching its zenith. Zenith: it comes from the Arabic for 'path overhead' and is normally used for when the sun is at its highest. I think it works for the breeding season as well – for when the skylark is at its highest overhead, showering song down on a marsh, above which gulls and terns shriek, waders sprint through mud, warblers racketing in the thickets. It is when the biggest number of breeding birds are still blatant: singing, displaying, foraging, where a lapwing will be somersaulting through the air, before activity slows down for the late-summer lull, the sudden secrecy that descends when birds have young to hide. But just as all waders like their marshes slightly different, so they all work to different schedules. Now is the overlap zone: some waders have young, some won't, some will still be passing through on their lengthy migrations to the furthest tips of northern land. And the result ends up like the scene of my dreams: my joy reflected in buoyant lapwings rolling through the sky, shining and whooping.

Wetlands are conservation's tool for fighting back. It has long been a habitat much easier to destroy than to create, but that has changed: conservation efforts have been focused on recreating these lost wetlands, most dramatically in Somerset, where results have been striking. Summer in Somerset does not resemble what it once was.

The Somerset Levels are one of the largest expanses of wetland in England, a heaven for herons. Dedicated conservation work has made it this way: old arable fields have become open-water wetlands, peat workings magicked into reedbeds. But this is not enough. These processes don't stop at the end of the reserve boundaries; birds don't fly only within protected land. The RSPB has designated the Levels a 'futurescape'; the Somerset Wildlife Trust prefers the slightly less awkward term 'living landscape'. The plans are similar: to join up the dots, to create a landscape-scale conservation effort, in effect placing the star reserves into a nature-friendly firmament.

I had wanted to meet Stephen Moss along a path on the Avalon Marshes, at the heart of the Somerset Levels, to discuss the changes he has noticed. Instead we email. Moss is the author of *A Sky Full of Starlings*, his diary from 2007 of a year's birding in his then new home of Somerset. It is a delightful book, redolent of the way that birds fold themselves into a real life, between work and children and the myriad responsibilities of adult life (it begins with him dressed as Buzz Lightyear).

Moss's first change doesn't surprise me. As well as the little egrets, which he describes in *A Sky Full of Starlings* as 'now as common as herons,'[8] he finds great white and cattle egret now easy to see, two more sparks of involuntary, Mediterranean surprise. Since 2010 these haven't been the only Mediterranean herons he has seen in the area either, but there have been little bittern, night heron, white stork and glossy ibis too. And it's not just the new species either. Over the same period, the great bittern has gone from a shadowy presence to fifty males, calling in spring as if they're blowing across the neck of an empty bottle from the deep of the reeds. That number is equivalent to the entire British population of calling males in 2007. For species such as the great bittern, long present in Britain but mostly on the edge of existence, a rare species of a transient habitat,* it has been a case of build it and they will come. The little bittern is a bonus: an opportunist in a warming climate, venturing further north than it has in living memory. Somerset is, it seems, the new Spain. In light of this and the conservation work in the area, Moss tells me that 'there will always be birds to see'.

Good news is always more noticeable than the bad, when you're on a nature reserve, looking for things to see – presence more tangible than elusive absence. None of the species

---

* Reedbeds have an unerring desire to become scrubby wet woodlands; a good and natural process, but not the open reeds that bitterns need.

he writes about in *A Sky Full of Starlings* has completely disappeared, although the chances of a sky full of starlings happening are fewer than they were; the presence of turtle dove, willow tit and corn bunting in Somerset now more of a question mark. It is a concern of his – and mine – that the new species colonising the area are almost a distraction; that the novelty factor of the unfamiliar casts a shadow over those that were more familiar, less attention-grabbing, and gradually dwindling away.

I'll leave the last words to him:

> Global changes to the climate and habitats threaten biodiversity at every level; and ironically it may well be the birds we once took for granted, like the swallow, that are worst hit. So, as always, I shall heave a sigh of relief every spring when the first swallows twitter in the skies above my home.

I am basking in this exceptional, early summer. It has hardly rained and it has not been cool in weeks. The days have been stuffy and muggy; they have felt as hot as at the height of July. Work continues, but the choice is either seeking to delight in the light and heat of it and work from the garden or hide from it in the cool of the shaded side of the house. Delight or suffering: the two available options for this current spell.

There is a sheer animal pleasure to these hot days; basking like a cat in a shaft of light or a fish rising to the top of a pond, the delight of being warmed through. There's also something unnerving about this heat, day after day, so early in the season. It's a little glimpse of the future: pleasurable on the day-to-day scale and worrying in the long run. But mostly the warmth casts a spell that allows us to ignore this; the threat remains abstract somehow, even if the symptoms of it are present here and clear to see.

I have been taking my mind off things with reading, but finding the heat penetrates even there. I have been reading Olivia Laing's *To the River*, her account of a journey along the River Ouse, from the High Weald to the Sussex coast, that she walked in midsummer, on days when the heat radiates out of her words and into my mind. Laing's walk ends in a birdless marsh, where 'the ground was bone dry and the reeds in their dank beds dipped and rose like a rusty ocean'.[9] But that's not the worst of it. 'I looked across the reeds to where the ruins were and saw an ominous glitter. A midsummer Saturday. It was going to be hell.'[10]

For me, marshes are more like heaven. Minsmere is where I had my Damascene conversion to birding.[11] These moments of conversion, these first life-changing experiences (though you don't necessarily know it at the time) are often so incredibly, intensely vivid, that they colour everything. I can't think of birding without thinking of marshland: water and waders and the way warm winter sunlight turns reeds golden, whereas in summer they are green and dense and full of birds, or the way that wind drifts through marshland, ruffling the reed heads into a sound like the flowing water that formed all of this in the first place.

I am fond of water and the way it comes and keeps coming, answerable only to itself, to its own fluid nature. We want to be near it – we build our towns and cities beside it. If we can't live there then we like to visit it. We build defences to keep it in its place. But water, like people, is not so fond of walls and restrictions and being kept in its place. We build where water wants to be and water will find a way to be there.

Bedfordshire is a county of rivers. It is a county of gravel pits. Everywhere in between feels like dry, arid lands. It lacks my marshy paradises. I have been crossing the fields at the back of the hamlet daily. When we arrived on the cusp of lockdown, expecting a temporary stay, winter was relinquishing its grip on the fields. The muddy footpath between the winter wheat and the ditch was drying out, the sparse green crop of the field didn't hide the birds of the old season: several hundred fieldfares, fewer redwings and a handful of lapwings, pulling up the worms and hunkering from the cold winds in the lee of the undulating ground. The fieldfares left shortly after, a big flock, their calls clattering as they headed north one afternoon, after which I saw no more. The redwings slipped away shortly after, unseen: there one day, gone the next. The lapwings just faded. A couple fewer every day until the barest handful, lurking in the grass.

The ground by mid-April was hard as concrete, the mud cracked and dried out as if it were the middle of a drought summer and not spring. There is a farmland reservoir where I count the tufted duck pairs. And then big fields of wheat.

The farmland reservoir is a raised square. You climb five paces up its earth banks before you can see the small expanse of water. Its banks are covered in ephemeral vegetation, the stuff that thrives where little else survives, though at this point in the season the vegetation is still lurking, not yet bursting up through the cracks in the mud. Despite this it is something of an oasis in this desert of wheat. The joy of a tiny wetland is this: for the species that don't want water, there is most of the rest of Bedfordshire. For those that do, there is less space, their habitat concentrated. Which means this tiny, sparse-banked reservoir can attract some unexpected species that drop in when daybreak interrupts their nocturnal migrations.

Each walk can produce a surprise. Due to the raised banks, you don't know it until you're there. Due to the small size, you can see everything in one go. Due to my almost daily visits, I know what to expect – and I know what I don't expect is a great-crested grebe. It looks too large for the reservoir; too sleek, too elegant for somewhere so rough around the edges. I have seen a great-crested grebe fly but only once or twice. If it weren't for that evidence I might as well think them flightless and this bird, here, something spontaneously generated: a feathered flowering. I walk around the banks and it swims on the far side, always leaving the maximum distance between us. It draws my eyes, even though it is a familiar species. Its presence transcends its place.

The next day it was gone. A few days later: a common tern. Migration is not always an end-to-end celebration of spectacular journeys by spectacular species but it's in these

moments, the common species turning up in strange locations, that the real magic of the workings of the world is
revealed.

The reservoir exaggerates what I am lacking. It's all the
standing water there is to be found. The ditches are running
dry under the hot sun. My walk, when I am feeling too lazy
to walk to the wood, circles these drylands: the cracked and
dusty earth of the green wheat fields.

The lapwings stayed in those dusty wheat fields. And
stayed. And from the garden I could hear the 'peewit' and
the 'pyewipe' and I just assumed they were late, or young
birds taking the year off. I assumed this all the way until I
was walking back down the road beside the field, near the
permanent puddle where a lapwing was. It called loudly on
seeing me and waddled off, an obvious, slow, noisy walk, the
sort that's meant to distract. Beside the puddle it left two
small balls of fluffy grey and white feathers. Lapwing chicks.
Tiny – a day or two old at the most, golf balls on legs. They
were slow on the uptake. A beat or two and then they were
walking off into the scant green cover of the wheat field. I
was gobsmacked. Partly because it seemed so wrong. Partly
because there are four red kites, a pair of buzzards, a raven
and a stoat in the area. None of whom would actively hunt
a lapwing, but all of which I thought would see a chick or
an egg or a nest on the soil and opportunistically take one.
A week later I find another one, the other side of the road
in a sheep field.

By chance, the hamlet is only a few miles from where
my great uncle was born in 1925 to the daughter of a village

blacksmith. Richard grew up in fields like these, before going on to a marvellously eclectic, over-successful life as a Bletchley Park codebreaker, bishop in Korea and an authority on hand-knitting. I remember him mostly this way: as an eccentric old man, the sort who moves to Cornwall and learns Cornish. When he died, he left us an incomplete memoir. In it he describes the Richard I didn't know, the one who grew up in Langford and Biggleswade, his failure to pass the eleven-plus and his alternative education in the fields.* 'Birds,' he wrote, 'were all but obsessive . . . I was allowed to walk alone and at will in these fields, always on the lookout for beady-eyed lapwings, the most lovable birds I knew.'[12] And Richard records his sadness, half a century later, when 'at the end of my time in Leicestershire, lapwings became much less common. But all things change constantly and people most of all.'[13] And when the memoir was discovered on his computer after his death, it was found in a folder under its working title: *Lapwing*.

I text my dad about the lapwing chicks. We share mutual amazement. And then he says, 'It was the sight Uncle Richard saw around Biggleswade. Brilliant they are still there.' And now the sight of that beady-eyed, emerald-and-white bird, with young in a Bedfordshire field collapses ninety years of distance between my great uncle and me, each one a reminder of a man I wish I had known better.

---

* Including how hares would eat the inside of a turnip and leave the skin whole.

Without Richard's memories of the lapwings in the fields around here, I wouldn't have known to expect them; I wouldn't have thought it possible, this far from a marshland. His phrase, 'all things change constantly', is important and true. It's how we adapt to that change that is important. These lapwings here have somehow adapted.

I am a pragmatist at heart. By which I mean hope is good; action is better. Reserves may be becoming islands in a sea of unsuitable habitat, but there are these small examples of lapwings making it work. The miracle of these Bedfordshire lapwings is that they're solving the problem without needing the islands of more suitable habitat. They're sticking it out in a modern landscape, with all the dangers that it holds, while our wetland stores carbon and holds water in the landscape, like an insurance policy for an uncertain future.

Birds have always held the capacity to surprise. The RSPB conservationist Dr Jennifer Smart says, 'It's unlikely that reserves alone will ever be big enough to protect wader populations.'[14] I agree. This is the reason why I was so delighted, in the dryness of Bedfordshire, to find those lapwing chicks. It was wheat and not grass, early growth and not grazed, not half a kilometre from the nearest woodland, farmland managed for money and not wildlife. Sometimes the birds find a way to make it work. This is not the new normal, but the old, before the shift to rarity, before their habitat became something specialist, before time and change overtook them.

Over the course of the month I followed the three from a great distance, watching as they grew ever larger, scampering over the short-turf sheep field, while the adults harassed the harassers – chasing crows, staring down sheep, escorting the kites and buzzards over the field at height and speed. My only reservation is a lingering uncertainty as to whether what I'm seeing is their final hurrah – the last of the local lapwings, nesting in the ordinary countryside, or if it's the start of a resurgence: the return of the lapwings, the redressing of the last few decades of wrong, a chance for normal to return to how it was before the baseline shifted.

Natterjack Toad

The Solway Firth is an amphibious place. A complicated mix of water and land. It so happens that this, the southern end of Scotland, marks the furthest north the natterjack toad comes in Britain. It is a species of edges: the edge of the country, the edge between water and land, the edge of knowledge.

Summer for the natterjack begins when the water reaches 7 degrees. It takes this temperature to coax a natterjack out of its burrow and to stir it into breeding. It begins with a croak – an almost onomatopoeic 'natter natter' sound. Historically their croak was the chorus of Caerlaverock: a sound that could be heard from over a kilometre away, on the still evenings when the Solway is calmed and sound travels from the shore to the hinterland villages. This racket lures the females in. Their spawn is laid in long strands that separate out into a single long string of eggs.

The natterjacks' habitats are ephemeral, their habits picky. They need their breeding pools to dry out but not while they are breeding. They need the grass by the edges to be short, for they run, instead of jumping, shorter limbed than the common toad. They like it if cattle keep the grass short but not while they're there for they can be easily trampled by an oblivious cow. They like the night – burrowing away into the soil to avoid the day's predators. Their fussy habitat requirements for breeding make a wader's look reasonable.

Earlier in the year, Dumfries had basked in the same rare start to the season: one of the warmest and driest across the country in memory, only this is obviously more outrageous in the west of Scotland. It worked well for the natterjacks: this drying-out is a sort of meteorological spring-cleaning that clears out the predatory larvae of diving beetles and the competition of common toad or frog tadpoles, which have the rest of the reserve's freshwater to breed in. Then rain, refilling the pools, gives the natterjacks a chance. And if you give nature a chance, it normally takes it.

It's hard to quantify, to keep track of tadpole numbers. But the thought on the reserve was that it was the best breeding season for many years.

And then came a spring tide. A spring tide is not seasonal but monthly, when the effects of the sun and the moon on the tide are working in tandem. The tide, aided by strong winds, pushed seawater all the way up the merse. I learn of this through Facebook. The Wildfowl and Wetlands Trust reserve at Caerlaverock reported their worries with a picture of the sea to within metres of the hide that looks over the merse. Normally the sea is about half a kilometre away. The natterjack ponds were flooded.

A week later. Good news. After the flood, came the rain: paths shut, wellies advised for walking through what remained open. Then, a toadlet: a picture on Facebook of a puddock in a puddle. The photograph shows water glistening, with mosses and reeds and other grasses suspended, a dense submerged substrate. On top, walking on water, a tiny purplish-brown toad, its eyes bulging, its skin shining and warty, the defining pale stripe down its back clear. It looks the size of my thumb tip. Jack, in animal names, is used to denote smaller size: this is a natterjackjack. A little hope.

Brian Morrell, the reserve centre manager, puts the picture into context for me. It is a case of shades of hope. He tells me that this year's optimism was borne on the back of six discrete colonies in pools across the merse. That there were an estimated thousand tadpoles on the reserve, which is great, and proof that, at the northern edge of their distribution, after years of meagre returns, they could still succeed, when things go their way.

The natterjack in the Facebook picture has limbs developed enough to run. It would have headed for the safety of higher ground, beyond the reach of the waves many times its size. Any late developers, any that were left as tadpoles, would have perished, washed away by the dumb luck of a big tide at the wrong time.

Morrell's assessment is that we ended up with a 'poor-to-OK' year, though it is hard to know what made it through. The toads' long lifespans mean we won't know next year either, the generations merging into each other, the poor years averaging out the great ones, the feast and famine of the tadpoles.

The worry here is that it has been famine far more frequently. Context contains unpleasant reminders of the current state of things. Before 2007, there wouldn't have been six colonies, but 150. There wouldn't have been a thousand tadpoles, but 150,000. The reasons for the crash are conjectured: Chytrid fungus, a doubling of rainfall here since 2000, the cumulative effect of storm surges like this one. No one knows.

The natterjack is a slippery thing: at the time of writing if you google 'natterjack toad climate change' then the first result is a BBC Nature blog from 2011 suggesting that the species will be a climate winner, that warmer Mays are beneficial for it. The result underneath it, from 2012, is a warning from the British Ecological Society that they are threatened by prolonged dry weather. Trevor Beebee, a former president of the British Herpetological Society, writing in 2018, thinks that the positive interpretations are 'unduly optimistic'.[1] Although there is one note of optimism that we know for sure in the natterjack's slipperiness. The Chytrid pathogen is currently present but benign in British natterjacks, for some unknown reason, despite causing devastation across the world's amphibians, implicated in multiple extinctions to the point where a *National Geographic* headline referring to it as the 'amphibian apocalypse' does not seem like exaggeration.[2]

Not much is certain on the frontline of Firth, the wetland where the complicated relationship between land, water and weather is vexed; where life for amphibians is subject to these fractious, changing forces; where summer is unsettled – and unsettling.

5

The Reaping

It doesn't see me until late.

I don't see it at all until it bursts out of the bush by my feet, a rupture of movement and fear out of a plain green hedgerow. In the split second, my birding brain grasps for details, something visual to cling to. Raptor, I think, as it bounds over and along the road at speed, a short distance for quick flickering wings. Then it lands in the light of a bare ash bough and turns its head. We go eye to eye. Its piercing yellow iris lights up the gloom of the murky afternoon. A little owl, as if affronted by my existence, glaring straight down my binoculars.

All owls have a facial disk. It can give them, at times, an almost human appearance. The little owl's face is flat at the top, fixed as if in a permanent frown. When alarmed, as this one is, it becomes like a furrowed brow, a glare communicating a message that transcends species boundaries. I almost feel like apologising. Instead, I lower my binoculars as it slips away further down the road, and through the hedgerow by the stable blocks.

Since lockdown began, I have walked the same routes through these farmlands since late March and I had not seen, heard, or come across any clue that there were little owls here. It is a useful corrective, for I had begun, mistakenly, to think that I now knew all there was to know about the summer birds of these fields. As I walk back, I realise I have no idea how to see the owl again other than by fluke. It's as if the species and I keep different schedules – hours, places – that only intersect when both of us are least expecting it. It's always useful to be reminded of the scale of your own ignorance.

There is an irony that it's the little owl that reminds me of this. It is not a bird here of its own choice but was the subject of repeated attempts to introduce it from mainland Europe in the nineteenth century before Edmund Meade-Waldo succeeded in doing so[1] – but it's also in the scientific name: *Athena noctua*. Athena from the Greek goddess of wisdom.

The little owl is a reminder of what we've done to the landscape. That lurking under everything is the influence of us. In the case of the owl, it's benign: they have been proved to have no discernible impact on the environment, as if they were always meant to be here; it was simply an accident that they weren't. Sometimes the consequences of our actions can blend in, can hide in plain sight (lurking behind a bole in a bough or deep in a bush, I bet), glossed over by the eyes or brain as something that's just always been this way.

Even here, the hedgerow and green farmed fields appear to have existed forever, as if formed millions of years ago, next to the geological feature of the cracked-edged asphalt of the road. Whether this is a positive or negative influence depends on your perspective: you might see this as a tamed and ordered land, the end result of the evolution of agriculture, from horse and hoe to our glittering utopia of expensive machinery. Or you might see this as a corncrake would, looking in vain for deep cover, places to hide because your habits match your habitat. To you this landscape is stripped bare and your world is turned upside down.

And we mourn your loss, even though the fault is ours and inevitable. We reap what we sow.

It is June now. I am beyond the top of that road, cutting along a bridleway between the wood and a wheat field. The day is still. The air sweaty, heavy with a sapping, lethargic atmosphere, holding me down.

A corn bunting flies from hedgerow to muckheap. It suits the muckheap better, blending in. Notoriously not much to look at, its plumage is brown and streaky, straw and twig and mud. A wattle-and-daub bird, the wattle coalescing to a big dirty splodge daubed on the breast.

The bunting and I are on the shallow crest of a hill. It begins to sing. My view is miles in every direction. His is along the verge of the track. Behind me the landscape ripples with texture – low hills and woods and church spires – and behind the bunting the muckscape, the pile of rotting matter, unwanted fibre, nutrients to return to the soil. In front of me the view rolls down to complete flat, the spread rug of Middle England: its fields and scant hedgerows as if drawn with a ruler. It's nothing like it was in May. Back then it was hot and the view clear; I could see the distant fields and woods on the horizon in what felt like great detail. June is sweltering, humid, and a haze has descended. Hay fever too. In May the view was rich with greens and swathes of blue when the flax was in flower. The roads were still quiet, lockdown still respected. In June it is beginning to go golden brown: the verge grass still struggling with the lack of rain, the barley fields turning the colour of lager. The grey clouds seem to exaggerate this colour. The horizon is faintly, ominously reddish under the clouds. Over the past few weeks things have got busy again. Traffic on these quiet country roads has increased. My attention is now divided between watching the hedges for birds and stepping into them, to get out the way of fast cars. But viruses don't respect a desire to return to normality. I fear what's to come.

The future does not look great for the bunting either. They are a relic of these farmlands, better suited to older agricultural methods, before modern machinery started to transform the landscape in the nineteenth century. They seem unable to catch up, sticks in the ecological mud. And summer is a pivotal time for them.

Summer is when other birds begin to stop singing, their breeding done for the year. The corn buntings are just starting. Their song is both strident and restrained. It's often likened to jangling keys but I find this unsatisfactory. To me it is like a stuck skylark. If a skylark song is like a rhapsody of delicate notes, then a corn bunting repeats a phrase of it, with an amateur's enthusiasm, as if it's perpetually practising to itself, but its song, like a human voice in a crowded room, doesn't carry. The strident notes seem to evaporate. Volume is not a corn bunting's thing. Its song leads to nesting: the average date for them to lay their first clutch of eggs will come only halfway through this month.[2]

Their summer is a slow one. It is by the middle of July that their first young will have fledged. Historically this would have been the first of up to three broods, of either four or five eggs, breeding by increments in the hay fields that would have grown long over the summer. But hay fields have, over the second half of the twentieth century, been replaced by silage, where the grassy field gets cut several times a summer. And the corn bunting, in its tightly woven grass nest hidden on the ground, can't cope with this. John Clare, who knew it as a 'groundlark', recorded it: 'Within a little bunch of grass / A groundlark made her nest', going on to catalogue the dangers of milking maidens and schoolboys who didn't know where it was, until 'when they came to mow the hay / They found an empty nest'.[3] Now, when the silage is cut the nest is not empty. We have known since the early 1990s that this a factor in the loss of corn-bunting nests and the shortening of their breeding season.[4]

Another study, from 1995, queries their struggle to adapt to these changes, concluding, 'It seems likely that corn buntings either evolved in rather stable habitats, in which habitat reassessment was unnecessary, or have difficulties assessing the future quality of a site: is this green stuff newly sown barley or grass?'[5] The former is the tantalising prospect: have they just fallen out of time? Are their slow habits an evolutionary hangover that has backed them into this corner? It would at least explain why they have remained here, in the winter wheat fields, around battered, scrappy hedges. I was almost as shocked when I first found one here as I was when I found the lapwings had bred: there's that gap between the ideal habitat and what they manage to make work that always surprises me.

The corn bunting flies from the muckheap to a hogweed in the verge of the track, carrying out the avian conjuring trick – singing from its perch on top of the three-foot-tall flower, which remains still, not bowing under the weight of the bird. That weight: 50 grams, a reminder that even bulky birds (18 cm in length and with an almost inflated look about them) are hollow-boned, solid yet somehow barely there.

Their attachment to place is legendary in ornithology. A look at the BTO's online report for ringed corn bunting reveals that we know of only one British corn bunting to have been found abroad (across the Channel from north Kent to Pas-de-Calais, a flight of 205 km).[6] Of the five records listed under examples of longevity (from five to eight years) only one was found somewhere other than where it was first ringed. Their slow habits are the anchor to the fields they were born in.

This stationary nature means they are one of the species that sings in dialects. A study from the north coast of Cornwall, carried out for eight years across a 14-km-long strip of coastal habitat, found that those at the top edge of the study area sang in a different dialect from those in the middle of the study area. Those at the bottom were again different.[7] Over the eight years of the study, they found only minor changes in the distribution of the corn-bunting dialects on the north coast of Cornwall.

That study was published in 1996. Cornwall was chosen because the nearest population of corn buntings was 160 km away: the chance of corn buntings coming from elsewhere was low, the Cornish birds effectively a laboratory population, isolated from the rest. The species that was once common in the county saw its numbers drop steeply in the 1980s until there were just fifty males left in 1991 living on the north coast.[8] The final sentence of the study states, 'If the decline continues then there is a strong possibility that local dialects could cease to be a feature of corn buntings in the UK.'[9]

It is a prophecy that hangs over them still as blogs report the continued destruction of their habitat. The corn bunting is on life support in Cornwall.

But the birds in the rest of the country have followed a similar pattern; the population has dropped by 88 per cent between 1967 and 2012.[10] Does the corn bunting on the Bedfordshire hogweed know this? Does it notice, over each of its average three years, slightly less territorial competition in its hedgerows, the increasing difficulty in finding a partner, the less familiar accent every summer? Or has the decline been too quick for the slowest of our species to notice?

I turn around, leaving the corn bunting to the lethargy of the still evening on the shallow hill, its jangling song still falling quietly over the track, back on its muckheap perch.

From here on, silence will reign: species after species will commence their only brood or their final brood, singing extinguished gradually, hedgerow by hedgerow. And farmland birds retreat from view, as deep into the shelter and shade of the remaining hedges as they can.

Mike J. Wareing was a farmer and an ornithologist in the 1970s who contributed to *Birdwatchers' Year*, a collection of mini-almanacs from 1973. He knew the value of his land, along the bank of Derbyshire's River Rother; he carried out the cost–benefit analysis of his hedges, the equation between lost land and wildlife habitat. He knew the history of it too: that his farm's Saxon name, 'Breck', meant 'wetland', that the neighbouring land was a medieval hunting lodge, that the oldest of his hedgerows dated back a millennium, and the value of kale to his cattle and his birds. He also knew his own complicity, when he sprayed pesticides, fungicides and herbicides on his cereal crops: 'There is no doubt that the use of them may have a far-reaching detrimental effect on the natural fauna and flora, but without their use it is doubtful whether even half our ever-growing population could be fed.'[11] Even a decade after *Silent Spring*, and despite the awareness of the problem, the reluctance to break free of the old ways still lingered; it makes me think of J. A. Baker and his insistence in *The Peregrine* of the birds that 'die on their backs, clutching insanely at the sky in their last convulsions, withered and burnt away by the filthy, insidious pollen of farm chemicals.'[12]

Despite this, Wareing's contribution to *Birdwatchers'*
Year is interesting for the dichotomy of what he managed
to find on land that did not promise much. The whinchats,
whitethroats and willow warblers he found behind 'the tip',
an area he describes as 'one of the most horrific witches'
brews of pollution and desecration'.[13] In an indication of the
difference between attitudes then and now, he tried to work
out its long-term effect on birds, instead of trying to fix
the brew. But perhaps it was the hands-off approach that
was working: wasteland is effectively a small-scale rewilding
without the hype. The scrub that grew back messily out of
the toxic ground was the reason for the birds' presence, in
spite of the pollution. The current national trends suggest
that the whinchats are now likely gone; the willow warblers
may be just about holding on.

Wareing also had corn buntings on his farm back then.
They are the first species on his list of those affected by
the disturbance of the intensive cattle grazing, which he
described as necessary to make money. He was sanguine
about it, pointing out the winter cereals that 'they are forced
to use' for a second nesting attempt.[14] This is where I feel
the gap of time. Now corn buntings are on the edge of their
existence in Derbyshire, clinging on in scattered locations
throughout Yorkshire. I wonder when the effect of that
intense grazing kicked in, when the corn bunting was lost
from Wareing's land.

I'm aware that I am just an armchair farmer: my acres are
mental and my crops are lapwing chicks and corn-bunting
nests, grown organically out of a healthy, perhaps Arcadian,

landscape. And in this Arcadian vision, I am the reclining shepherd, enjoying the fruits of unseen labour. Farmers of course don't have that luxury. But it's hard to ignore the effect our industries are having on the land.

As with the corn bunting, so with the curlew. In his book *Native*, Patrick Laurie talks about the sad fading away of curlew from the hills of Galloway, his hill-farm wader of choice. Known traditionally as whaups across Scotland, we see them mostly as winter birds of coastal mudflats and saltmarshes now but they were once common in summer. Their numbers have dwindled with the piling up of each failed breeding season as pine forests are planted on old farms; as modern machinery thrashes them out of the hills.

In his June chapter, Laurie talks about finding a pair of curlew chicks: vulnerable, fragile, unfathomable, defenceless: 'I was utterly drunk on those two youngsters.'[15] And our heart breaks in July with his, as each chick turns up dead.

Sometimes walking in Bedfordshire can feel like walking through an old landscape painting. Something like Thomas Gainsborough's *Mr and Mrs Andrews*, where his high-summer scene is wide and open and green. It was painted in 1750 when Gainsborough was just twenty-three years old. In the painting, the couple are in the foreground, Mrs Andrews on a bench and Mr Andrews holding a gun and wearing a tricorn hat. Some of the details (the hat, the gun, the breeches) are very of their time. What is interesting to me are the ones that haven't changed – their dog, the wheat, the sheep, the gate and the lack of hedges. It is a portrait of enclosure: this is not common land. John Berger sees it as 'exposing the arrogance of the land-owning classes of that period'.[16]

I agree with Berger's view. But my attention is drawn deeper into the landscape than the people in the foreground. There once would have been birds. These fields, in the low-intensity farming of the time, would have been full of the riotous birdlife of southern English farmland in summer, when the harvest has disturbed the insects and the birds profit. There would have been corncrakes and corn buntings skulking in their camouflage, yellow wagtails scampering the field margins, red-backed shrikes impaling beetles into their thorny larders. Gainsborough does not record any of this in his painting. Perhaps there is no room for them because this abundance of birdlife would have been obvious, in the way that normal things are so frequently unremarkable. Or perhaps they would have been too full of messy life in a painting that lacks it: the Andrews and the landscape are neat and ordered and deeply clean. Even the trees, with crisp light falling through their leaves, are neat. The dog is looking up at its owners with a fixed, lifeless gaze. Mr Andrews looks bored. Mrs Andrews looks slightly to the side as though she does not want to be there. The sole exception is a small white weed poking up near the edge of the wheat stooks: a small interruption of real life into the scene.

Mr and Mrs Andrews is a very English picture and Bedfordshire is a very English landscape. Walking through its countryside these days, it's possible to feel as if you could be anywhere in the south, with its gently crumpled undulations, the green trees that seem to make up the horizon anywhere away from the towns, and the wheat fields in every direction. It's a landscape for the middle ground: the view is never wide enough, never grand enough for the sublime vista. The foreground is bare, and the reason for the view is that the hedgerows that should be in the way have either been obliterated by the intensification of farming or are so sparse in cover they hide nothing. The middle ground, between undulations, might have an attractive manor house to remind you that this landscape is owned, or an attractive cottage, thatched and white-washed, to remind you that the workers in the fields can't afford the houses of their forebears now.

The landscape is as picturesque and as unnaturally neat as it is in Gainsborough's painting. And at the roadside, the wheat and barley that have escaped cultivation are growing bigger and healthier than they are in the fields, before the flail comes along and obliterates the entire verge to a grassy stubble.

Birds have been a redeeming feature of this static scenery. Although I see a landscape completely opened up, farmed to the seams, sprayed and flailed and neatened, the space and food for birds gone in the name of efficiency, the species that suffer for this are still present here, hanging on in their vestigial numbers. On one walk I disturbed a grey partridge that shot up by my feet – startling me – and it quickly put most of the field between us in a frantic blur of wings (91 per cent decline between 1967 and 2010).[17] I have seen a sulphurous yellow wagtail patrolling a set-aside field that the farmer had sprayed with enough chemicals to turn the grass peroxide blonde (45 per cent decline between 1995 and 2012).[18] I have seen a family of mistle thrushes in a battered hedgerow (52 per cent decline since 1967),[19] a cuckoo stringing its web of calls from the tops of the spinneys (65 per cent decline since the 1980s).[20]

It was the first cuckoo I have seen in two years. The first yellow wagtail in three, corn bunting in four. I saw a grey partridge here at Christmas, but before that my previous one was so far back in time I cannot precisely place it, but I suspect it was the best part of a decade. And this feeling is incredibly complicated for me. I'm excited, as birds always make me; I'm delighted to be seeing these species when I had begun to wonder if I would ever see them again. But here is the kicker: it's one pair of yellow wagtails, one individual cuckoo, a few pairs of corn bunting, I do not see more than three grey partridges at any time. The species might be here but their numbers are low, the birds being spread ever thinner. And it feels as if I'm writing my own archive of loss, walking through a living museum before it's sealed off behind the glass case of history, a display of the future dead and gone.

There is one species whose absence I've already noted: turtle dove.

I haven't seen one since 2016. They were in the countryside around me where I grew up, but they just faded away. The farmland lost them, then the local nature reserve followed. I stumbled across some on the Suffolk coast but I couldn't repeat the trick, same place, same time, a year later.

Suffolk and Essex hold, according to the RSPB's 'Operation Turtle Dove', 30 per cent of all the turtle doves remaining in Britain, but my experience of trying to find them there is not positive.[21] And now I live where they aren't found, and I have no idea where to find them; it feels entirely possible that I'll never see one again.

The era of turtle doves has passed. It would take a miracle to return.

At least it doesn't elude me in print. *Wilding* by Isabella Tree is a rare optimistic story, relating her hands-on role in the pioneering rewilding of the Knepp Estate in West Sussex, and how nature bounces back when given free rein to return to a place managed by pigs, ponies and cattle, behaving as their wild forebears would have done. From a starting point of none, they had sixteen singing male turtle doves by 2017.[22] Watching one, through her binoculars, Tree feels it is 'caught . . . in the crosshairs of time, a thread from the earliest books of the Bible to the tales of Chaucer and the sonnets of Shakespeare intersecting with our world at Knepp'.[23] And I am green with envy.

The rot set in in the 1970s. Since then, the turtle dove has declined by 98 per cent. Breaking it down further, a little over half of Britain's turtle doves disappeared between 2012 and 2017.[24] The trajectory is incessantly down. The RSPB and the BTO agree on the causes. It sounds perfectly obvious but the birds are not breeding as much: fewer young, raised over a shorter period of time. The reasons are habitat loss – the weedy margins, and big hedges in farmland – and from that, a lack of food. They prefer to feed on seeds in the breeding season and our neat, tidied countryside doesn't have this any more. We are starving them towards extinction in Britain.[25]

I don't really know how to process this, how to grieve for something going, not gone, the suspended sadness of the inevitable. Perhaps anger at how it got this way is a more honest reaction. Aldo Leopold wrote that 'we grieve only for what we know'.[26] I'm glad that I knew them.

It's with turtle doves in mind that I walk to the farmland reservoir. It's not a happy walk. The reservoir banks are basically bare earth; they have been bleached with herbicide and given an agricultural buzzcut.

Over the spring this was greenery, and became, earlier this month, a profusion of ephemeral flora. Poppies and thistles and plants I don't see enough to get to know. Linnets (70 per cent decline in England since 1967)[27] and skylarks (63 per cent decline in England since 1967)[28] fed among them, a valuable source of insects and seeds and cover. Dragonflies: emperors and black-tailed skimmers perched among them. Damselflies: small red-eyed, azure and common blue did too, as well as lekking mayflies. None of this is perhaps very exciting but it's very necessary. Insects, after all, power the natural world. Now all are gone from the banks.

A picturesque landscape is a lie. Around the corner a farmer has shot five crows and strung them up on a fence. The fence runs across the middle of the field and I cannot ID which crows they are, strung up with their wings out, heads slumped, like fallen angels. I suspect they are rooks. Rooks are plentiful here, the spinneys studded with their nests, the fields echoing with their *craa craa*. There are jackdaws too, brilliant exploiters of the farmyard spills, the gaps in the buildings. There are carrion crows and ravens around as well – agents of mischief, if mischief is merely making the most of the mess we wish to forget. There is no reason for any of these species to be shot, no reason for the reservoir bank to be scalped.

There is a precedent for my turtle dove fears.

When Charles St John wrote, 'Oftentimes have I opened my window during the fine dewy nights of June to listen to these birds as they utter their harsh cry in every direction,'[29] he was talking of the corncrake. That harsh cry is the only exception they make to a life lived in otherwise perfect secrecy. Their calls are onomatopoeic of their scientific name – *Crex crex* – an unusual quirk in nomenclature that records one of three of their distinguishing features. That *crex crex* is insistent and loud, sometimes maddeningly so. Frequently described as rasping, it can sound like an electrical short-circuiting, or a rattle or a ratchet. Its rhythm is mechanical, incessant, its tonal quality that of something breaking or jamming or jarring. On the island of North Uist, where traditional hay farming still exists, *crex crex* can still be heard with a backdrop of perpetual wind and waves crashing ashore, corn-bunting song and lapwing calls.

When I was there, it was the corncrake's second defining feature of which I was most in awe. Standing by the fields of Balranald, hearing them, thinking about them. Corncrake plumage is best described as cryptic: a mottling of browns, blacks and greys that becomes a medley of shadow, vegetation and earth. They are cryptic in another more basic sense for a birdwatcher like me: they are almost impossible to see. They live in fields where the grass is longer than their bodies. They slink, skulk, always resolutely hidden by the greenery. If they move their heads while calling, it makes even pinning down which corner of the field they're in tricky. And then a head popped up between two wind-blown dock leaves. Shaped like a teardrop, in grey, brown and pink, it went *crex crex crex crex crex crex*, vanished, popped up a few dock leaves down and did it again. And after watching greenery for hours, it was brilliant – relief and exhalation and exhilaration. One of Britain's most elusive birds, finally seen.

The corncrake is also one of Britain's rarest, in part because of this love of hiding.

There were once many across the country, when we lived in the era of the scythe and hay-making was common, when the landscape was grassier and taller. Cutting hay with a scythe is a slow and laborious process, moving from one side of the field to the other. This gives corncrakes plenty of time to slip away from field to field, hiding in whatever greenery remains uncut. Despite being migratory, flying annually to Central and Southern Africa and back, they seem not to trust their wings over short distances. But this reluctance to fly, or even leave the shelter of long grass, isn't a problem when you can outpace a figure with a scythe.

The corncrake is not a species to which time has been kind. To be more specific: the twentieth century was when the species vanished from most of Britain. The advent of the combine harvester was the real killer: chasing the crakes and their chicks through the cover, until the last of their habitat is cut and the crakes have nowhere else to go. A love of secrecy, in the modern age, is a death sentence. There's a simple process at work here. Mowing a field from the outside in and finishing in the middle surrounded by cut grass is lethal to the corncrake. A figure of 55 per cent of corncrake chicks die this way.[30] Mowing from the inside out allows the birds to escape.

By the end of 1977, there were only two pairs in Bedfordshire, both recorded as 'probably' breeding. By 1992, there were only two pairs in the entirety of the Thames and Chiltern area: a huge swathe of southern England from Bedfordshire and Hertfordshire across to Oxfordshire. Things were less severe in Scotland and by less severe I mean that between 1972 and 1979 more than half of their corncrakes vanished; but at least Scotland still had some.[31] This contraction has continued. In Britain it is now found almost exclusively in the archipelagos, a bird of Orkney and the Hebrides. This is their third defining feature. For England – and for most of mainland Scotland as well – they are gone and a return looks unlikely. It has become a bird in the past tense.

The last time I had a near-encounter with a corncrake I was in Westray, Orkney. I walked past a silage field, the grass grown long in the unusually hot spring we had that year.

Crex.

It was a single call, then silence. My ear caught the sound too late. Two steps beyond, I stopped and spun on the spot. And I waited five minutes before I heard it again.

Crex.

I traced the field with my binoculars, heads of grass and dock and dandelion waving in the breeze. It wasn't a surprise to not see it. But it was a surprise to hear the next *crex* from a wall. I scanned and traced it to a single starling.

Starlings are capable of long memories for sounds that they can repeat. It was mimicking the corncrake that was once in this field and is presumably there no longer. So I don't know if it was from last year, or generations before, but this is the closest I have come to a corncrake in the decade since I saw that teardrop head between the dock leaves of North Uist. I came close to a reproduction – the past-tense bird.

I have to remind myself that it's not all gloom. That reaping what we sow is a good thing, if what we sow are the good seeds.

In Cambridgeshire, the next county over from here, the RSPB runs Hope Farm. It is them putting their money where their mouth is: a wildlife-friendly farm that turns a profit, while pioneering methods that help our farmland birds, such as leaving parts of the fields unsown, or changing the rotation of what is sown. Ten years after the project began, they had a 200 per cent increase in breeding farmland birds and a 1,000 per cent increase in wintering farmland birds.

It makes a profit of £40,000 a year but, more importantly, holds grey partridge, lapwing, yellow wagtail, corn bunting. 'Hope' seems an entirely appropriate name to me.[32] We can get back to ways of farming that turn a profit, while leaving space and food for nature. Hope Farm is proof that it can be done in the intensively farmed south, in a place where space is at a premium and the logic of economics holds sway over all. Space can be created for the slow lives of corn bunting, while still producing food in a modern way, without reverting to the nineteenth century.

A few days later, I stop at the top of the road from where I encountered the little owl. A Chinese water deer – not a planned introduction as the little owl was, but a species that escaped from Woburn Safari Park's collection, forging a new feral population across eastern England – is staring back at me from a green field. A buck with a small and dog-like face, given away by the fang-like tusks that sneak out of his mouth like antlers in reverse. A cyclist pulls up too, takes a drink as the deer bounds off through the field, a small beige body disappearing.

'Did you see that hare?' says the cyclist.

I explain. He seems interested to learn a new species. And then unprompted he says, 'I've cycled down these roads every day in lockdown. It's been great to see the changes, to see spring properly, things growing, birds singing.'

And all I can think is amen.

Solstice

It is 20 June. We sit out late. A leap-year solstice: not as warm as it has been, not as sunny as it could have been, but it feels as though there is nothing else to do. So we may as well stay out, making the most of the languorous solstice hours: luxuriating in the English peak of seventeen hours of daylight, while knowing that in Dumfries, at this time of year, you can look north up the Nith while walking home at midnight and still see light in the sky.

This moment is the beginning of astronomical summer. The place where I should really have begun, although meteorological summer suggests it should have been the start of June. Realistically we don't measure summer by these rigid definitions. A hot day in late April or May, the sort that feels blisteringly hot in the context of the days that have come before, rather than the days that are to come, is the beginning of summer, a simple, pagan-ish calendar of light and heat. The official definitions of summer turn it into a time of stasis and decay. If summer begins today, riding in on the solstice's daylight high, then all is downhill from here.

I'm lucky to be here, I think, as I sit out in this wild garden, the feathery leaves of the ash turning gold in the last of the light, the horse chestnut similarly burnished by the leaf-miner moth. To be taken into a family, to be temporarily stuck in a new place and to begin to consider it, in idle moments, home, or at least as homelike as anywhere else I have been in my last decade of unintentional transience. I never thought I would consider this place home and it surprises me that I feel this way. But my resolve is to live more like the horse chestnut, at home no matter where it comes from, rather than the larvae of its leaf-miner moth, which hollows out the inside of the leaves until they fall prematurely, weakening the tree: its habitat, food source and home.

The solstice is not the zenith but the turning point of the year. The early energy that coursed through me, that sent me out for daily walks, has subsided. It's an annually repeating pattern: my own personal solstice. Right now I am lethargy and shortening enthusiasm. I'll get over it but a gentle melancholy has taken its place instead. As if I have to have a purpose now, as if I can't be outside for the sheer pleasure of it. I haven't been able to face going back to the reservoir, to the only decent patch of water in walking distance, since the banks were trashed. I don't want to walk up the road and see the black flags of strung up crow corpses.

Instead I make do with the lesser stag beetle that walks through the evening, stumbling between plant pots, waving its thick-ended antennae above the tiny brackets of its jaws. Yellow shell moths flit along the long grass and hide on the underside of leaves. The setting light intensifies the colours of the surviving bee orchids. I have been tracking them in the garden since I first noticed their rosette of green leaves in April spread across the wilder corner, from right under the pyracantha's protection of thorns, to the middle of the sun-parched lawn. I noticed their mid-April blackening at the tips from an unexpected frost. I watched as the leaves that form a sheath to protect the stem raised themselves up, and the rosettes grow, right up until mid-May when the lack of rain began to parch and bleach and kill off the ones in the lawn.

Half died. All of those with the promising beginnings died. So I was delighted by the seven that survived to flower this June. The falling sun catches its star-shaped collar of lilac sepals. In the middle, the labellum, the part that attracts insects for pollination, is yellow, maroon and red, arranged in a pattern that is supposed to (and apparently does) resemble a bee. The shape of it has always resembled a particularly manic-looking rubber duck to me. It glows. Unseen to me are the allomones it will be exuding, chemical signals that deceive the passing bees into attempting to mate with it.

I'll miss this.

Light falls. The temperature slips. We move indoors.

It is time to return to Dumfries. Lockdown in England has dissolved, with or without the government's help; whether it's due to rogue trips to Durham, law fatigue or crisis fatigue, the yearning for normal life to return has resulted in recklessly packed beaches. The parks are packed too: litter left in huge quantities, fires caused by barbecues, illegal raves. It reminds me of isostatic lift: land rising up after a geological weight has been removed. It's as if some people, having deemed the weight of the pandemic to be lifted, have risen up wildly, indulging in their worst habits, as if, having left no trace since late March, they must now leave a huge one to make up for it.

Lockdown in Scotland hasn't dissolved. But it has slackened a little bit, the first step on the road to reopening. The five-mile guideline for movement is weakened. We take the opportunity to return: from a Bedfordshire morning where a fierce heat burns from a pale blue sky above bleached brown road verges, to a Dumfries where the sky is silvered with drizzle. We've dropped 10 degrees in temperature from the start of the journey to the end. There's a moment on the main road into town from the east where the road clings to the side of a hill, and the cattle fields fall away like an opened curtain, revealing Dumfries in the valley, below the dark lump of Criffel, and the forested ridges of smaller hills and the vivid greenery of the farmed fields around. It is a reassuring moment. The right decision has been made.

We get out of the car. Breathe in the air. Soft and clean. It begins to drizzle as I haul bags inside. The neighbour sees us over the low garden fence.

'It's a bloody mess.'

And in that moment I don't know if he's talking about our garden, the government or everything else right now. I assume our garden. But what is a bloody mess to him is, to me, a wonderful profusion of fox-and-cubs, hawkbits (I am not good on round yellow flowers), bramble, rosebay willowherb, and the star: a single, white common spotted orchid, the small flower held within the foot-high riot of grass. Despite the drizzle, a small ringlet butterfly flits from flower to flower, not waiting for the perfect moment but making do with here and now.

We had missed Scotland. It feels good to be back.

6

Silence Descends

High summer is a time of silencing. Individual by individual, species by species; the task of territory holding and finding a mate has been completed. Feathers are worn and in need of moulting, young are in need of feeding, the hot sun beats down on opaque leaves and birds move to the middle of bushes, deep in the cover or high in the tree canopy. Each species falls quiet or irregular. The exuberance of life before has become almost distracted, as if July is a season within a season: the time between the singing and the pre-migration activity, when birds seem to vanish. It is an avian solstice, when the old bird of spring gets ready to renew itself, to become the bird of autumn, ready to head south.

It is the worst month for birding and my attentions turn to other fields of natural history. But in town there is still birdlife to be seen; while I am walking the streets of Dumfries and the backways on its periphery, the flitting swallows and house martins hold my attention, the constant motion hypnotic, a reminder of the energy that came before the summer pause.

Back home we try to reorient ourselves in our surround-ings. The route is familiar, the weather as I remembered it. Walk out of the flat, down through the cemetery to the river and cross the small bridge over the Nith. A choice: we turn downriver, follow the bank past the cricket pitch and the allotments towards the quay. We walk alongside the scrubby field, set aside for the river to flood at high tides, behind the small skate park. It's a walk we've done countless times since we came to Dumfries, our fresh-air constitutional, our auto-pilot walk, while our heads can be elsewhere. This evening has a deep grey sky and a slight breeze threatening squalls of rain. This is not a walk for fun, just a walk to get out of the house. I do not bring my binoculars.

There's no need to think until we get to the scrubby field. Rosebay willowherb flourishes here on land without an official purpose, where it can grow without permission. It grows in thick stands, blooming with four pink petals on each flower, a spread of flowers around the stem. The stem is a wick that burns pink as the plant flowers upwards. On its own, one is a nice splash of colour. In this field they grow in patches but with a density that paints the green field in bands of hot pink. But we are not quite there yet. They are just flaring into flower now, a week or two later than they are in England.

A few minutes further down the path and my ears engage. A familiar buzzing is coming from the field. A grass-hopper warbler, singing, though singing is perhaps not the correct word because it is more like the hum of a pylon than any noise a bird might make. It is a constant and continuous metallic ticking, an unspooling fishing reel of sound. No variation. No pausing for breath. No change of pitch or note or pause, only volume when it moves its head, throwing the noise in different directions. This is familiar for me: I hang about in the habitats they like, the wet and the lush and overgrown. It is more familiar than the sight of them, for grasshopper warblers are less famous among birders for their improbable song than their invisible habits.

Another squall of rain. The warbler gets louder. I curse not having my binoculars.

Grasshopper warblers have spent nearly the entire twenty-first century on the red list of conservation concern as their numbers in Britain dwindle. It's hard, with such a secretive species, to work out how many there are. The method is to count the singing males: in 2016 there were 12,000 holding territories.[1] Fields like this on the edge of town, where the grass grows long and the flowers are thick in summer, let them hold territories after their migration from West Africa, hidden in the depths, singing unseen – the way they like it, one of the curious species that sings all summer long.

The rain gets harder. We cut the walk short. The warbler keeps singing.

I appreciate the ceaseless efforts of the grasshopper warbler. Because, without it, these walks would be almost totally silent, beyond the rain dappling the leaves, the wind clattering branches, the ever-present squawks of gulls or the screams of swifts.

Silence is a haunting thing. Summer silence particularly because it performs a trick on us. It seems as if things drain away at what should be, according to our human calendar, the height of activity, when the breeding birds should be flourishing; it's as if we turned away for a moment and when we looked back, they had vanished. As if the entire season had disappeared, a reminder of the dead days of February when you can go outside and see nothing at all. We could mistake it for a sudden absence of life, if we didn't know that it's not the case. In reality it's like a sort of aestivation* – a regathering or regrouping, away from the heat. Things get better at hiding, horizons shrink, not unlike the state of the roads at the start of lockdown, when our temporary silence enabled us to hear the sounds of nature better.

The silence masks the genuine absences. When it seems as if all birdlife has vanished, it's easy to forget that one species really has. At the start of July there were at least three cuckoos in East Anglia. Four days later two of them were in France. By the fifth day, the third had joined them there.

These three cuckoos are bearing trackers. A project that the British Trust for Ornithology has run since 2011 has been catching male cuckoos – bigger, more able to bear the weight of a GPS device than a female – and tracking them on their migration to Africa and back.[2] Although as a statement that is the wrong way around. They are essentially a species of the edge of Central African rainforests that migrates

---

* The summer version of hibernation.

north to Britain to breed. One of the cuckoos, named Chris, was tracked by the BTO for four years: he spent 15 per cent of his time in the UK, 38 per cent of his time on migration and 47 per cent of his time in the Congo.[3]

They are the first of our summer species to leave. Their biology enables the adults to do so as soon as their eggs are laid, leaving their young to be raised by whichever unfortunate species has unwittingly ended up with them – often birds that are a fraction of their size, needing to stand on the baby cuckoo's back to get close enough to pass it a beakful of insects. With their young taken care of, cuckoos have become notorious for having one of the briefest stays in Britain of all our migratory breeding species. It's almost as if they sense the solstice, then immediately flee from it; they anticipate the closing-in of the evenings, the gradually lengthening nights and they are terrified of what this means: the slow slide to a cold and hungry autumn, discernible to them even now in the height of heat, the longest days of summer.

We've understood since the thirteenth century that the cuckoo is the herald of both summer and autumn. There's an old song, 'Sumer is icumen in / Lhude sing cuccu',[4] that celebrates the cuckoo as a harbinger of the good weather and the growing season, the time when life would be perhaps a little easier than the suffering season of winter. This is what seems to have crystallised in the public imagination – there was an old tradition to write to *The Times* announcing the first cuckoo of summer being heard. Sadly this no longer happens, yet the legend lives on: *The Times* called the book of its collected correspondence *The First Cuckoo* (the sequels were the *Second, Third* and *Last Cuckoo*).

The less frequently quoted penultimate stanza is 'Cuckoo, cuckoo, / You sing well, cuckoo / Never stop now.'[5] The author must have known that by the time they stop singing, they're already slipping away, heading south, heralding autumn. We share the cuckoo's fear of the end of summer. The last stanza merely repeats the words 'sing' 'cuckoo' and 'now'. It doesn't specify whether it means the male's double-note singing of its name or the female's giddy bubbling reply. I think it might perhaps be the latter: the heady repetitive reverie of the ending fits their unrestrained song.

At some point we seemed to forget all about this tradition. Or maybe we didn't forget exactly, but took it for granted, stopped bothering to notice. It's only now when the cuckoo's heralding song has become so rare that we are paying attention to it again, truly understanding what the cuckoo's movements mean.

We are not cuckoos. Miranda and I are not so nomadic (not so parasitic either, I hope). While cuckoos migrate, we stay. I am reminded that ecology has its etymology in *oikos*, the ancient Greek for 'house'. Our understanding of nature and our surroundings begins at home. But while it's good to be back, we are still dealing with that sense of dislocation, disorientation; we are disconnected from what should feel like home. The last three months in Bedfordshire don't feel real. Now transplanted into what feels like a different season,

I'm relearning my route, walking my way back around the roads again, remembering where everything belongs in our kitchen cupboards (it's amazing how the banal drops out of your head when unused). Freud had a word for this: unheimlich, the feeling of the strange in the familiar. We need to rediscover our local patch, our garden, the parks and streets, to find out what happened while we were away for the first half of the season. We need to readjust to the rain and grey that is reminiscent of when we left, in March.

It rains all week. Returning home in the height of summer and it's the rain that helps most of all: familiar Scottish summer rain, missing from our English spring, helping us reconnect with the expectation of place.

I am thinking about this while it chucks it down outside, my lockdown cyber-birding habit continuing even now we are allowed to go out further afield. The sky a symphony of greys and gale-force winds and if you told me it was a warm November day I would believe you. Such is summer here. Tracing the season is difficult in town. Brick, concrete and glass are hard surfaces, unchanging with the season, not the way that the leaves of a tree bloom and subtly change over the course of the year, hardening, darkening with the summer. Towns are built to shelter us from nature rather than bring it in: I am grateful that Dumfries is small, that a river runs through it and that the edges are permeable and that wildlife finds a way to slip into our urban setting.

When we returned home, I was delighted to see swifts again. They were present in rural Bedfordshire but scattered thinly, the habitat not ideal for them there; the eaves of the housing estates here are a better fit, where they find small crevices to nest in, the straight streets seem to compel them into racing at top speed, their screaming calls sounding as if their flight is a rollercoaster only just within their control. Wherever I have travelled in Europe, this has always been the case: anywhere we have erected buildings, swifts (common here, pallid in Portugal, alpine in Greece) take up residence. Common swift pairs for life, which for these birds could be up to eighteen years; their existences are at once fantastically different from ours and startlingly similar.[6]

We've shared our houses with birds like these for centuries. Now they seem to be leaving home. Common swift in Britain declined by 57 per cent between 1995 and 2017.[7] Modern houses, or renovations to old buildings, lack the crevices under the eaves that they require for nesting. Changes to our homes evict them from theirs.

It's the same story for another house-dwelling species of summer, the house martin, another insect-eater. Their decline is more climate-related: requiring rain in spring to make mud available, which they mould into nests on the side of buildings, a habitat that brings them into conflict with the neat and tidy habits of homeowners. House sparrows have declined hugely as well. The traditional species that we used to see are disappearing, brick by brick, taking their familiar chatter with them.

More summer silences turning into permanent absences. Sound is I think my worst, my dullest sense, yet it is incredibly important. There's a sort of grief reported by ageing ornithologists who can no longer hear the highest pitch of bird sounds, like grasshopper warblers or goldcrests, effect-ively losing them these species. That sadness is coming for all of us.

We woke up to rain on 15 July, St Swithin's Day. It had cleared by the dregs of the morning's first coffee, but the sky spent the rest of the day swithering between rain and not rain. The weather forecast gave only a light chance of rain for the rest of the day, but my eyes disagreed – the sky that ominous shade of grey, the clouds swollen and bulging but resolutely not bursting. The forecast tells me something else as I flick through the rest of the week ahead. Here, over the third week of July, we shall lose nine minutes of daylight out of the evenings, eleven minutes out of the mornings.

Town feels closed, as silent as the birds. Where I work is still shut and the pubs are too. Some shops are open but I don't want to go to them, to run any unnecessary risk. So I don't, and for the first few weeks of being back, I don't walk into the town centre. I regret this, partly because with-out exposure to people and crowds I find it easy to regress into the part of myself that naturally recoils at this, and partly because early July is my favourite Dumfries micro-season. It is the season of just-fledged gulls. It is the time of lesser black-backed gulls contemplating pub doors, looking through boutique windows, walking around the fountain on the high street, as if perplexed by life, wings and their new surroundings. Gulls trying to enter pubs is one of the quotidian surrealisms that I have missed this year (replaced by the new necessary horrors of face masks, R numbers and Zoom calls). By the time I feel I can venture into the town, when the need to visit a shop becomes too pressing, this year's quota of young has already graduated from the street to the river, each standing on a stone, looking as though they know their wings and their way around.

Downriver. Miranda and I return for another evening walk, binoculars brought as an afterthought. I have been conditioned to not seeing anything in the quiet time of July but I don't want to miss the grasshopper warbler again, or anything else that might be lingering. It has been a mild day, not a warm one, weak sunshine lighting the willowherb, the field pinker than before. Rosebay willowherb is known as fireweed for being the first plant able to grow back after a fire has devastated all that grew in a field or wood. But it works the other way too, for the flaming pink is setting the field alight, the flowers a little higher up the stem than they were. It's not a plant that requires bright sunshine: it makes its own light.

We amble along the riverbank, the Nith at a low ebb, a handful of goosanders asleep on the mudbank of moulting ducks, shed feathers floating in the water. It's a languid time of the year. Lethargy reigns.

The grasshopper warbler starts reeling, a sudden jolt of energy. I look in its direction with no expectation, anticipating the normal invisible singer. But then I think I see it, perched on the top of a head of willowherb, a dark blotch in the pink. It must be something else. I double-check anyway.

The *Collins Bird Guide* contains an outrageous slander. The first sentence of the guide to grasshopper warbler identification describes it as 'grey-brown bird with no striking plumage features'.[8] If that were the case, I would be peering at the blot trying to resolve some certainty from it. Instead I know instantly what it is. Olive-brown and streaked all over the back that is turned to me. Wide at the front end, its bill wedged open and turned up, broadcasting song to the silent field. Wide at the diamond-tipped tail. It turns to face me, to unleash its torrent of unreal, unreeling song my way. The breast is paler and plain. It is striking for a warbler – you don't need to be a connoisseur of shades of brown to see it either. There's nothing in this country that matches it for tone, streakiness or shape.

I hand my binoculars over to Miranda and she agrees. After I spent half of our previous walk downriver talking about it, she expects it to be dull but says it is surprisingly elegant. I find it electrifying. This is not a once-in-a-lifetime view, but still rare, perhaps more like twice a decade; the sort of unpredictable encounter that makes a summer. I see grasshopper warblers so infrequently that while their song is a part of the soundtrack of summer wildlife, something that blurs into the background of other, more obvious species, I can remember each one I've actually seen.

I picked up a book from 1946 in a charity shop: two quid well spent for the Eric Hosking photographs, from a time when bird photography was challenging and Hosking was the master of the birds at the nest, birds with young, birds on a post with food photographs. It's impossible to over-emphasise how revolutionary these were for the time. Looking back now, it makes the early twentieth century look like a time of unimaginable fecundity: the birds are all well fed or busy feeding young, while the static style of the images makes it look as if the birds are giving a knowing, side-eyed look of exhaustion at Hosking's camera.

The actual prose of the book was an afterthought. *Our Birds Month by Month*, by Gordon Hamlin, an author I know almost nothing about other than this was his book with the least twee title (*Nature Parables* and *More Nature Parables* are the others listed at the front). The content is clichéd and pedestrian, and sometimes imagination intrudes on evidence, giving a clear idea of attitudes to nature in the 1940s. But it's nice to know that some things haven't changed since then: 'Silence begins to steal over the garden when June gives place to July. At first we wonder what is missing to make the garden seem so empty and evenings so forlorn. Then the fact strikes home – the blackbird has stopped.'[9]

One of the reasons why silence has always descended at the height of summer is moult. Moult is exhausting, the intensive act of a bird replacing itself, feather by feather, often changing plumage: the bright feathers of spring gone (although for certain species, including starlings, they stay the same – the shiny feathers of spring are those of autumn, with the dull tips worn off).* It is what ornithologists would

---

* Feather moult is an exceptionally complicated subject and this is a very basic summation of it.

describe as 'resource intensive' and why when natural food is at its peak, birds seem to vanish. It is what Hamlin describes as their time of 'dishevelled apathy', a phrase that toes the line between anthropomorphism and playful description.

But his July is not totally silent. He is obsessed with hearing those that haven't quite stopped singing yet (as I guess I have become obsessed with the grasshopper warbler), mapping out the persistent yellowhammer, tree pipit and blackcaps.* What is noticeable is that much of Hamlin's birding takes place around his garden, as if he too needs to reorient himself between a spring and autumn spent exploring more exciting habitats; his garden goldcrests a palate cleanser for the dog days.

This is not to say that Hamlin has nothing to tell us about how birds have changed. We return to lapwings, the unanticipated totem of our spring. Hamlin is out for a walk in an unnamed place (though the foreword suggests it's somewhere in southwest England, somewhere warm, where spring and summer come early). In his avuncular way, Hamlin 'obeys that old rule of ours . . . leaning upon the topmost rung of a well-worn stile', when he spots a family of four lapwing chicks, a handful of days old. This seems incredibly late, about as late in the year as it is currently possible for a lapwing to breed. But these days birds are breeding earlier than ever: perhaps the chicks I saw in May

---

* The tree pipit is a proper birder's bird: the features distinguishing it from meadow pipit are very subtle. So Hamlin is quite probably a more serious birder than his prose style suggests.

would have been exceptionally early then, as Hamlin's now seem exceptionally late.

There's another change. A subtle one, noticeable from an earlier paragraph. Hamlin describes July as the time 'when the lover of field paths and byways is often brought to a halt by the many delights of colour and form'.[10] And I have lost count of the summer paths I have taken by fields that are monotone now – the blue-green shine of perennial ryegrass or the beer-brown barley fields – the colour and form of wildflowers lost to the search for efficiency and the application of herbicide.

A thing about summer, generally, is that the middle of the day is usually rubbish. The light is long and the action compressed to either beginning or end. Midday, midsummer, is a time of secrecy for most birds. As well as moulting, it is a time for raising their young, which are blundering about the insides of bushes, hidden by the dark shadows of opaque leaves in overhead sun. As the month progresses, my bird obsession falters, briefly. Staring at shadows is not fun. I begin to look for other things. This month a comet is burning a brilliant arc through my social media.

Comet Neowise is one of those classic examples of the baffling scale of space. It is 64 million miles away. We discovered it only at the end of March and by the end of July it will fade from the night sky, and be gone for at least another 6,000 years. It was formed shortly after our solar system, a glitch of rock and ice thrown into the great nothing of space, as if it were a deleted sentence from the editing of the beginning of everything.

It is a one-off on the tiny scale of human life: the sort of thing that innately defies attempts to understand it. I don't need to understand it: knowing about it is enough and I know I would like to see it, to be in the presence of something beyond my comprehension. Day by gloomy day, I can't look at Twitter and Instagram without seeing pictures of it: a magnesium-bright blot and a kite's tail of dust and vapour trailing through the darkness. More skilled photographers picture Neowise in the night sky behind famous landmarks. My friend Chris gets it above the Stour estuary, flat calm and shining with the last of the light.

A week after the comet sweeps the internet, I see a chance. A day of patchier weather, some breezy blue skies blowing in between rain showers. An hour before dusk and it's looking good: only a couple of clouds visible through the window. The sky is a cool blue and the colour leaching with the light, down the plughole of the day. By the time it's dark enough to try, I step out into the street – slippers and a fleece and binoculars – and see a bank of thick dark cloud to the north, the exact direction and height I have been advised to look at. I wait. A hedgehog, the first I have seen for several years, scampers across the road with surprising speed, the claws tapping noisily on asphalt. I scan the sky with my binoculars anyway (hoping the neighbours don't misconstrue my interest in the celestial), tracking across the distant glimmers of light above rooftops. I see several stars and a plane and dazzle myself on a streetlight. I give up.

My dad sends me a photograph of it with the outline of my grandma's house underneath.

Two nights later, another light evening. It begins with earth's comets: the swifts. As July draws on, the flocks become bigger, bolder, louder and lower for reasons that are unknown to me. Now they form a tightly balled flock, joyriding down the street, skimming the garden fences, and from our first-floor flat window, I look down on them, their bow-shape black wings impossibly thin, impossibly fast, their shrill voices screeching through the window panes. And it lasts until dark, and they disappear, either roosting under the eaves and gutters, or asleep on the wing, high up.

Not long after, the stars come out. And so do the clouds. It's as if they have read the same websites as me and know that now is the peak time. It really is amazing how when all you need to do is look north, then north is the only direction in which there will be thick cloud cover. There is always a moment of suspense involved. Our door looks to the south: I need to walk around the side of the flat for the inevitable disappointment. But I hang around at our door tonight.

Two bright stars are aligning in the southern sky along our street, one above each terraced side. I bring out my birding scope, hoping again that the neighbours don't see me. I line it up: taking bearings from the church spire, the big leylandii tree, avoiding the street lights, finding a small speck of light. I twist the eyepiece, zooming in. The speck increases in size. I fiddle with the focus wheel until it resolves out of fuzz. A burning bright white dot with a ring around it. Saturn! I pan to the right, to the other bright star: no ring but a line of four white dot-like moons running each side of it. Jupiter! And despite the fleece, a shiver passes through me.

That my small, cheap birding scope can collapse an incredible distance, the millions of miles of darkness that separate me from these points of light, into clarity; that it can bring the planets, quite literally, to my doorstep, worlds where a single season lasts three years (on Jupiter) or seven years (Saturn)[11] is astonishing. It's not often you get to experience the sense-defying sublime in suburbia, the heavens from our housing estate. A reminder that things exist beyond these terraces. Birds link me to the world, but the night sky extends that, taking me from this small corner of town to halfway across our galaxy, through sublime silences, away from known life, reminding me of the smallness of everything on earth. I feel connected again, oriented at last.

Nightjar

Evening closes around us, the sudden onset of clouds killing the late light and scattering droplets of rain. We are ten minutes from sunset but it is an atypical evening for here, where the light normally lingers late. Sunset – grey, going greyer – could have happened any time in the last hour.

Growing up in Suffolk, I would leave my search for the nightjar – the most improbable, elusive bird – for the hottest evenings of June, the cloudless days when it would be over twenty degrees at dusk and moths would rise up and float like dust in the forest stillness. If I waited for one of those nights here then the year would pass by. Today has been the warmest day of the week, a rare dry day. July is spinning on. If the moths can cope with these conditions, I can learn to make the best of what we have on this dark night.

Moths do not get the night to themselves; they are the indicator that what I'm looking for could be nearby. Nightjars are the avian equivalent of bats, hunters on warm nights of the rising moths and beetles. They are fully nocturnal and plumaged like pine bark and forest floor, so that when daylight returns, they just melt away unseen. This window between dusk and total darkness is our only chance to see them.

Into the fading light Miranda and I walk out, along the path between the peat bog and the pine wood, the heather seamlessly merging with horizon. Colour has been drained: it is as if we are walking through a greyscale landscape, speckled with white bursts of cotton grass. The path turns into the pines. Heather spills from the bog and fills the space between trees. Bracken scents the air. The path is narrow and twists between trees whose roots kick out, trying to trip us up. The further we go, the more the blaeberry fills the space on the floor of the wood where neither bracken or heather grows. In the gloom the berries shine blue, alluring but bitter, still a few weeks from ripe perfection.

Walking out of the shadow of the wood is like going back in time by ten minutes. It is lighter here in the clearing, light enough to pick out the details, the succession of the habitat, from where the young birches grow on the edge of the wood to where they fade out in the water, peat and heather of the bog. Moths, small and pale ones, species with identifications that elude me, flutter up from the heather. The nightjars will not go hungry tonight. A big frog hops through the undergrowth, stops and vanishes, its camouflage aligning perfectly with the broken twigs, heather branches, dead grass. Bats flicker overhead. A young tawny owl shrieks from deep within the trees. And we wait.

Nothing happens. Or rather: moths continue rising up, while bats patrol back and forth along the treeline. The air smells fresh but the sense of impending rain is getting stronger. A few late crows sail over towards their roosts, calling loudly, and the brightly lit tractors rumble down the minor road beside the bog. The sky incrementally finds new shades of ever darker grey, imperceptibly until it takes you by surprise and it's nearly 10 p.m. and time is running out before it will become almost impossible to see. And still there has been neither sight nor sound of nightjars.

By now the middle of the wood is almost totally dark, gnarled branches looming at us, visible only against the crack of pale still in the sky. Against the soil, the roots tangle, still tugging at our feet. It is only the density of the undergrowth that keeps us on the narrow, twisty path. A single, late-to-roost robin calls, shuffling along a dark branch.

By the bog it is too dark to see the cotton grass. Only the pale shards of tree stumps stand out in the lingering grey. Yesterday's was a new moon and today's sliver has no power to penetrate the cover of the clouds. The result is almost total darkness. As we wait, the first of the midges investigate my ear tips, while the bats start circling low overhead, spooling thread through needle-straight pines. The farmers are talking in the fields at the far side of the road, their voices carrying in the stillness to the trees that surround the bog like a hand cupped around an ear.

Light fades to almost night.

And then it just materialises. Buoyant wings raised, barely flapping, the nightjar drifts in out of the darkness, flies around our heads and silently slips into the trees. It perches briefly, its flat body pressed horizontally across the branch, its big head held like a gnarl in the wood. Then off again, another swoop and circle of us, flashing the white – an impossible, almost luminous white – in the wing tip and tail that tells me it is a male.

Nightjars are like nothing else. That is to say, if you didn't know they were a bird you could jump towards supernatural explanations. They look flat and stiff, somehow flying without flapping, wings held high, seeking out moths in the darkness, to bounce into their bristle-bracketed mouths. The tail is long, the feathers held together, thin and straight. Their plumage is of the earth, but when they fly they are anything but.

We are spellbound, held in silence. It swings around again, uttering a quiet bark-like call, before vanishing into the dark.

Vanishing is their story in Scotland. *The Birds of Scotland* records them as present and common across the country in the nineteenth century. By 1981, the first time a figure for Scotland had been reached, it was a population of thirty-three males singing, in only twenty-three locations.[1] The retreat into Dumfries and Galloway was almost total. They are doing time in the pantheon of Scotland's incredibly rare breeding birds: rarer than golden and white-tailed eagles, capercaillie and snow bunting.

It's hard to get a handle on their numbers. Like most nocturnal birds, you can count them only by night and by sound, and it is only the males that sing their otherworldly churring song, so a partial figure is all that's possible. In 2016 that was forty males in the Dumfries and Galloway night. By 2019 that was fifty (for this year, alas, no figure). They are still in that pantheon of rarity but consolidating; their nocturnal magic is holding on, holding steady.

7

Fluctuations

While the birds hide at the height of July, my mind wanders towards another of summer's defining spirits. *Psyche* was the word the ancient Greeks used for butterfly or moth; it also meant soul, which feels appropriate for the transient, hard-to-grasp nature of a butterfly flicking through a meadow, or a moth passing within the light of a window at night, elusive and intangible.

They are essentially the same thing. Or rather, butterflies are a small subset of the Lepidoptera, almost all of which are moths. For every textbook definition distinguishing butterflies from moths, an exception can be found.

Although some species of moths can be found in the winter, the majority fly in summer: butterfly numbers are at their peak in July, the most species on the wing in the summer heat. While some of them are vanishingly rare, and disappearing fast, others are thriving. Some species are helped by the changes to the season, enabling them to spread to new territories, or their numbers to boom; others have successfully adapted or have responded to our efforts to save them. The pressures facing day and night, young and old, generalist and specialist, are different, and each species shows us a different way to understand what is happening, how our insect life is being affected by the changing summer. And there are some lessons to be learned from the success stories. It's not enough to outweigh the declines, but it can be a welcome relief from the onslaught of bad news.

The gravel track snakes steeply up the side of a burn that runs clear and quick off the hillside. Mabie Forest is fresh with the scent of pine, the clarity of morning sunshine and the calls of robins beside the path, alerting the forest to my presence. Mosses are glistening, emeralding the tree trunks, and small bonnet mushrooms are beginning to grow next to the bracken after the summer rains.

At the top of the slope the forest opens up, revealing a meadow, grass cascading back down the hill. I step briefly into the sunshine. Underneath the long grass, the spangled stars of lesser stitchwort, sky-blue speedwells and yellow buttercups. Grasshoppers are stridulating from the depths of the grass. I raise my eyes and the grasses take on a velvet-like appearance: the lengthening summer shimmer of seed heads all the way down the slope, back towards the woods. It's the same pattern on the far side of the valley, dappled with drifting cloud shadow and the horizon fading out in a haze. Orange butterflies bring me back. They flit through my vision: large skippers and small heaths. But the orange butterfly I am looking for is not here and I am pressed for time twice: the forecast gave me a window of only a few hours of sun this morning; and it is late in the season for the butterfly I am seeking. I carry on.

The fritillaries are a family of butterflies that, in a class of insects of supreme beauty, look as if they have been fashioned out of stained glass. The pearl- and small pearl-bordered fritillaries are typical: a luminous deep sunset of orange, suspended in a filigree of black lines.

The underwings are the best way to tell the fritillaries apart. The butterfly habit of feeding on flowers means you need to get down to their level to get a good view, bent as if in supplication to the clover, violets or trefoil, to see them. The pearl-bordered's underwing has a row of white spots at the rear edge of the hindwing – the pearl border – and two pale panes inside. The small pearl-bordered has more pale panes inside and a row of black studs in from the pearls. These are more useful distinctions than the half-centimetre difference in size there is between the two species.

Pearl is the butterfly of May: I have written that one off. Small pearl-bordered is the species of June: as it's already early July I am covering the ground quickly, hoping beyond hope that if there's still a small orange gem fluttering from flower to flower, this will be the way to find it.

The twentieth century has not been kind to fritillaries – they are some of the rarest species, specialists of woodlands, with very specific dietary requirements, breeding just once a year. Studies have found that single-brooded butterflies tend to be harmed by the seasons changing earlier; if the conditions aren't right, they don't get another chance, unlike the species that have several generations a year. And it tends to be worse for those that also need a specialised habitat, as the pearl- and small pearl-bordered fritillary do, and cannot leave in search of better grounds.

Inside the forest is a small reserve that Butterfly Conservation keeps especially for these populations. It is helping kindle them back to a stable state, a small area of old woodland managed the old way in the middle of all these pines: an oasis of the right sort of violets, the right sort of light, the good springs. The sides of the reserve's tracks run dense with brambles and thistles, not only a rich source of pollen but the armed guards of botany, sheltering the important plants these butterflies require – from us, deer or other herbivores – behind a fence of thorns.

After a quarter of a century of monitoring, Butterfly Conservation and Forestry Land Scotland are confident the population of pearl-bordered fritillary at Mabie Forest has become one of the biggest in Britain.[1] What is good for the pearl is good for others too: twenty-three of Scotland's thirty-two species can be found here on this south-facing sunny ribbon of grass between deciduous trees.

But this is not the time to rest. This is a small conservation success story, and it has taken twenty-five years for this reserve to get where it is. For the success story to be anything other than small, this recovery needs to be replicated across the country. They have had an encouraging decade; figures show slight increases in occurrence and a larger increase in abundance, though these are very small steps. If we take that time period back to 1976 the data still shows a 95 per cent decline in their occurrence.[2] There is more work to be done.

The path crosses the forestry track, heading uphill. The ground here is a swathe of clear-felled forest. Opening up the ground means foxgloves proliferate, weaving pink lines through the grey remains of timber, soil and rock. Out of the wood's shade, the day is warming up, the bracken radiating the heat back onto the path. I am marching uphill but all I see is small tortoiseshells, another orange butterfly that quickly raises and then dashes hopes. Small, but not small enough – yellow, blue and browns mixed in with the black lines. It feels churlish, they're lovely – but I am focused. Fritillaries or bust.

The way down from the hill takes me towards the furthest point of the walk. Mud path joins forestry track. Gravel underfoot, wide enough to send timber lorries down, but permeable for wildflowers at the edges. A shock of orange catches the corner of my eye. It disappears behind a bush. It comes back again, descending to a red clover. Fritillary! That familiar stained-glass pattern. The shade of orange that makes other butterflies look dull, sombre by comparison. I think I know what it is but I double-check, dropping to my knees on hard stones. As its proboscis searches through a pink clover flower, it flicks its wings: my head to the hot ground, I can see it, almost like the upperwing in negative. Squares of white instead of thin black lines. A scatter of green scales instead of orange.

Dark green fritillary might not have the rarity and the fractured distribution of the pearl- and small pearl-bordered fritillaries, but it is nobody's idea of a consolation prize: gleaming and big and precious, they are the sort of insect that makes you stop and look and grin. I can't speak for the scarcer species. But the fritillaries I have seen, the commoner ones, have all been strong-winged species, quick-flying and flitting and able to put distance between me and them in a flash. The shimmer of green is as good as it gets before it is gone.

On this bright forest track anything flying today would be out in the sun, of this I am sure. And I am not short of others in this butterfly haven: peacocks, small tortoiseshells, ringlets, meadow brown and more dark green fritillaries, big and bright and bold. One female, her colour slightly duller, her black markings smudged at the edges, is crawling deep in the undergrowth, her abdomen curved down away from her legs, laying eggs in the matted vegetation below. A male floats down the path like an autumn leaf.

I have run out of time. Clouds are forming, the forecast rain looming; the butterflies will soon sink to the depths of the vegetation, to ride out the rotten afternoon. I am a day, a week, perhaps a fortnight too late to find the small pearls; a month too late for the pearl-bordered fritillaries. But the absolute grace of being a naturalist is this: there is no wasted time. Even though I didn't find the fritillary I was looking for, I have spent the morning in a special patch of woodland that is unlike most others around here, where a space for wildlife has been made, catering for their specific needs; the sort of thing we never used to need to do but that is now top priority if we want to see this recovery continue.

Butterflies are easy to go looking for: they just need a sunny day. Moths are trickier. They came into my life by accident: a buff-tip, a moth that looks like the tip of a birch branch, on the white-washed wall of a campsite toilet block; an angle shades moth that looks like a withered leaf on a front door; a lime hawkmoth in the hands of a school mate who went behind the bike sheds and got more than he bargained for. Spectacular species, caught out by poorly chosen roosts, sleeping and still, trying to go unseen. Often they did. It wasn't until I met Andy – owner of the equipment that lures them out of the night – that I found moths properly.

I should be in Norfolk now. Andy and I should be standing just back from the beach, staring at the light of a moth trap, as many naturalists across the country do, spending the short summer night wondering what is hidden in the surrounding darkness. A moth trap is harmless, its principle simple: a container filled with loosely arranged egg boxes and a strong light bulb suspended above. Switch it on at night, turn it off at dawn and root through the boxes, where the moths lured in by the light will have settled in the crevices. The harsh light of a moth trap casts everything in a pallid glow, reminding me of a line of Keats' 'Ode to Psyche', with its 'pale-mouthed prophet[s] dreaming'.[3] We in turn dream of what the box might contain – Psyche's cryptic creatures, with names like incantations: blood-vein, engrailed, dark dagger.*

* Keats, *Bugs Britannica* suggests, knew that psyche meant both soul and moth; literary history does not record whether he ever stood around a moth trap with a group of naturalists.

I have a hate–love relationship with moth-trapping.

It begins with hate. Cables that need untangling, plugging in, extension leads wrapped in plastic bags (the high-tech approach to not electrocuting yourself with the fall of the morning's dew). I am also a reluctant riser with the sun. Regularly I oversleep and miss the unboxing of traps. Four in the morning is a different country and no quantity of coffee will get me there regularly. And when I do manage it, I am bleary-eyed, half asleep as Andy and other friends switch the lights off, dismantle the trap, and fish out what is inside.

Sometimes there is nothing. Sometimes there is a gem. You never know what's going to be in the next egg box – Andy's mantra, the drive that has kept him trapping regularly for the past twenty years.

That is the love part. I remember one July: red underwing, black arches, tree-lichen beauty and the dusky sallow. A red underwing is an espresso shot of a moth. Big, bark-patterned on the forewing, flashing hindwings of bright red and thick black lines. It wakes you up for the black arches, one of my favourites: bright white in the light of the trap, a haywire of black lines, white legs, black feet, black knees. The tree-lichen beauty and dusky sallow are closer to the classic moth: crumpled patterns modelled on dead leaf, bark, scraps of moss, a delicacy in miniature that would be easy to pass off without a closer look. It's the key lesson that moths provide. Always take a closer look, even if it's only for the beauty.

I had wanted to track down the hyper-specialist scarce pug of Norfolk. It requires sea wormwood for its caterpillars to eat, while it flies across a tiny percentage of England's east-coast saltmarshes at night, vulnerable to its coastal habitat being ruined by stray high tides. But the scarce pugs will have to wait for another summer. Andy and I go mothing by email instead. It's better for sleeping patterns, at least.

We reminisce about our first Jersey tigers. We both remember those moments well. Andy on an August dawn in his garden, in 2009, perched on the outside of the trap. He tried to put it in a pot for a close examination: he fumbled, it flew, landing in a neighbour's leylandii. So, in the first light of morning, he was up a ladder, wielding a sweep net, retrieving it from his neighbour's garden. Mothing requires determination. My encounter was simpler: a colleague walked past a buddleia bush near the office one lunchtime and came back brandishing a picture, innocently asking, 'What's this?' I shot out the door.

Moths named after other animals are exciting and aptly named. Fox moth is a nice fluffy, rufous species. Lobster moth is better, for its caterpillar has a threat defence display that involves folding itself up like a crustacean. Hawkmoths are big and bold, origami-winged and impossibly bright colours. The tiger moths are stunning: black and any combination of white, yellow and red arranged in striking patterns. The Jersey is a particularly smart example. The forewings are night-dark, split by lightning bolts of white: the hindwing reddish orange or yellow, with a handful of black ink blotches.

The next summer I didn't need to run out of the office to see one: it flew in through the open window. We then bumped into them all over my corner of suburban west London. This felt extraordinary: the first stirrings of an influx, irruption or a consolidation. The Jersey tiger had been in London since 2004 but with almost overnight ubiquity, it felt as though something special was happening in 2014. This species was, hitherto, confined to a small handful of locations in England, mostly in Devon – the Isle of Wight was the closest to London they were found.

Six years later they had reached Norfolk, a spread so thick and fast it's almost breathtaking, and driven by climate rather than any other change, the increasing warmth ushering them up country. For some species, the future looks bright. Over a forty-year period to 2010, 160 moth species increased, with the Jersey tiger in particular 'a real attention seeker' in Trevor Beebee's phrase.[4] The kicker: 260 species of moth declined in the same period. The garden tiger moth: upperwings like a Friesian cow, underwings a vibrant coral with cobalt spots. Ninety per cent of their old numbers have gone from England, and this loss seems to be concentrated in the south and at lower ground: it's as if the warming climate is giving us a live demonstration of its effects, replacing one species with another. It's a message, should we choose to comprehend it. The meaning of it is that we've lost sixty-five species of moths from Britain since 1900.[5] That's more species of moths lost than we have species of butterflies regularly breeding here.

The comma is a butterfly that's almost as luminous as a fritillary: the incendiary orange scales of its upperwings are dappled with black; its tree-bark-patterned underside notched with a single pale comma-shaped marking. Despite their name, they have not paused or taken a breath recently. By 2010 they had spread north in Britain by 200 km in twenty years,[6] one of the most dramatic examples of a butterfly taking advantage of our changing environment.

They were once restricted to hop plants as the food source for their caterpillars. Then, perhaps driven by the dwindling British hop industry but for reasons that remain unknown, they switched to nettles, the ubiquitous verge-side plant across the country. And their populations boomed. This is good news, not only for the comma, but for us: the joy they bring, wrapped up in their beauty, their incandescent orange scales, is now easier to find throughout the country, a common sight at the right time of year in the right place. And the right place has gone from being just the Welsh borders to almost all of the country, as far north as Inverness. If we could work out why their caterpillar food plant changed, we'd be closer to knowing why some species can adapt and why some species get left behind by environmental change.

The red admiral is darker than the comma. The red of its name is restricted to a vivid band on each wing, against a backdrop of black-brown, with white notches and a single small sky-blue spot at the bottom of each hindwing. It is a striking common butterfly. I feel compelled to photograph every one I see, which means in summers like 2019, when migratory butterflies such as red admiral and painted ladies are everywhere, my phone fills up, my progress on any walk is slow, distracted and bent over buddleia or this-tles. Migration for a butterfly is a seasonal get-rich scheme. Year-to-year changes in red admiral numbers here are prone to the fluctuations of weather and the fickleness of their migration and breeding success. They follow the warm weather north over the course of a year, breeding where they go. Each generation develops quickly, moving north, laying eggs, repeating, until the end of summer, when the movements turn south, back to the Mediterranean.

Or this should be the pattern. Warmer winters have enabled red admirals to start spending that season in the south of England. A head start on summer. In good years, such as 2017, this head start lets them boom: Butterfly Conservation's annual summer survey found a 75 per cent increase on the year before. In 2020 they were the sixth most common butterfly, although their numbers were down by 33 per cent from 2019.

They are not the only migrant that seems to be turning resident. The clouded yellow, a small, rich golden-yellow, molten-butter butterfly, that lives like the red admiral, spreading north, breeding and carrying on, is also showing signs of setting up resident populations. They are a species at ease most of all in the Mediterranean, but August on the chalk grass downland of southern England resembles their erstwhile home. I have even fleetingly seen one in Galloway.

The warming summer can get more beautiful, more joyous still. Swallowtails from the European populations are showing signs of supplementing our relict population in the Norfolk broads; long-tailed blues have bred on the south coast, and large tortoiseshell seems to be attempting to recolonise after its extinction here in the 1960s. Purple emperors are bouncing back too from their stronghold in English woods. Not only is the warmth helping them, but an increased understanding of the importance of sallow trees in their life cycles. They are the most spectacular species of all, though when I saw my first I did think it was a Cadbury's Dairy Milk wrapper for the size and iridescence of its purple flash.

In his memoir *The Moth Snowstorm*, the environmental journalist Michael McCarthy writes that humans are hard-wired to find joy in nature – in its presence, wildness and aesthetics. He notes that not everyone feels this way but those that do feel it intensely. As McCarthy puts it, '[We find] ourselves on a planet that did not have to be beautiful for us to evolve on it, but turned out to be beautiful beyond what, in a monochrome world, we might ever imagine.'[7] Purple, yellow, red, orange, black. All these butterflies are bouncing back, or consolidating, or changing in ways that leave us with more beauty, more pleasure in our countryside, more colour on our sunny summer days. Climate change has facilitated these butterflies in the hard work of adaptation. The future might hold entirely new species spreading up from the south, following the movement of their needs. The worry is what happens when ours need to carry on heading north, beyond here, too.

We want increasing numbers and spreading distributions. But sometimes we need to be careful what we wish for. Not all new species are welcomed with open arms. Not all are good news.

One species Andy and I trapped together in the west London wood was an oak processionary. It is a species that was new to Britain in 2006, first discovered in a housing estate in suburban southwest London. It is quite a smart-looking moth: fluffy, silvery-grey wings, three dark grey lines boldly wavering across the wings. It is entirely innocent. It's just that in its earlier stage, as a caterpillar, as far as humans and oak trees are concerned, it is a lout. Oak processionaries congregate, en masse, where they eat the leaves of oak trees at night, by day proceeding back to their nests with the tight choreography of a military parade. If disturbed, their hairs can be an irritant, capable of penetrating human skin and with the potential to cause intense itching or dermatitis.[8] It was actually this – an outbreak of dermatitis in an apartment block – that led to the discovery of the country's first colony.[9] When we caught it eight years later, efforts to stem its spread across London were just beginning.

Our habit of moving trees across country borders is leading to the spread of these invasives: animals or fungi that find themselves in the wrong place, behaving in ways that are entirely natural to them but wreaking a disproportionate havoc on places not prepared to receive them. *Chalara fraxinea* is a fungus that causes ash dieback disease; it is currently swingeing its way through the canopy of British ash trees. It was brought here in imported trees. Grey squirrels harbour squirrelpox, a disease that has backed the red squirrel into remote corners of England and

Scotland. Escaped mink are bad news for a large amount of our aquatic life. It's not their fault; it's ours. We seem to have been historically lax with biosecurity measures, and the consequences can be far-reaching, hard to control and sometimes irreversible. Those that are tasked with stemming their spread resemble King Canute; armed with chemicals and traps but still overwhelmed by the tide.

These species have ways of going rogue: while it is our actions that have been causing the spread of the oak processionary moth across Europe, there is evidence that the negative effects of these rogue outbreaks are climate-driven and becoming increasingly common and acute.[10]

Across Greater London, efforts to stem its spread are still continuing. The method of control is chemical. Another friend of mine, who wished to remain anonymous, serves on the committee of a charity-run London nature reserve. In 2014 the Forestry Commission visited with an official order: that they were to carry out surveys for the caterpillars, and that if it was deemed enough of a problem, they would use pesticides. The reserve was happy to open its doors to the surveyors but not happy for the pesticide (normally *Bacillus thuringiensis* – a bacteria that paralyses the digestive tract of insects, starving them to death) to be used; the lessons of *Silent Spring* run deep after all in the conservation consciousness. Despite the presence of the caterpillars, the Forestry Commission has not yet required the use of chemical control on the reserve (as it does elsewhere). One factor my friend gives is that caterpillar numbers are much lower on the reserve than in a nearby park. He suspects that this is to do with nature's own biological control. The reserve has plenty of nest boxes and a good population of blue and great tits making ready use of them; helping, he suspects, to keep the oak processionary numbers down and the reserve chemical-free. Meanwhile the oak processionary moth continues to spread.

Not every new arrival is an invasive. Many arrive and have no deleterious effect, such as the little owl, or at least no fatal effect, like the horse chestnut leaf-miner. The nature of an island is one of influx and invasion, colonisation and extinction. Our duty, as the species capable of causing and hastening this, is to have as light an impact as we possibly can, to avoid having to resort to chemical solutions.

The old lepidopterists who described and named their study subjects were more flamboyant than ornithologists. Where birds can tend towards brown and prosaic, butterflies and moths have a spirit that seems to transcend that. Even if they are also brown.

The Scotch argus (and the unrelated brown and northern brown argus butterflies) get their name from Greek mythology. Argus Panoptes was a Greek giant with a hundred eyes: the name Argus has fallen into everyday use most frequently as a name for local newspapers across Britain, a sort of synonym for 'observer'. It suits these butterflies, speckled with fake-eye markings down their brown wings, but the only one I have seen before was flighty, nervous, difficult to get close to, as if those eyes were real.

I am walking on a track through the Galloway forest, towards the moors, and I need to keep my argus eyes down for frogs on the path, up for birds in the high trees and sky, to the side and ahead for deer crossing, butterflies flickering and dragonflies zipping along the forest edge. The sun is pure, the temperature rising.

It takes a few miles of walking through the quiet forest before we reach the moor. Once there, we immediately find a small and dark butterfly. It lands on a thistle by the track with open wings, a stripe of orange on each, holding a line of white dots inside black spots. Scotch argus! These are hardy butterflies, not the brightly coloured admirals and tortoiseshells that decorate delicate garden plants at the height of summer days. A cloud briefly covers the sun and it drops down into the grasses. The cloud disappears and the argus goes with it, zipping off over the trackless bog.

We carry on. The OS map suggested the habitat was better a little further on, where the track emerges from the cutting to trace the contours of the land around the slope of Airie Hill, through a patchwork of moor and pine forest. We didn't even need to get that far. Another Scotch argus was feeding on a thistle by the side of the path, wings shut, its proboscis fishing around each pink frond of the flowerhead. It might be peat-dark on top but its underwing is a sunset of bronze, an orange sun with a pair of eye markings, a broad sweep of silver cloud. I inch closer, slowly leaning in with my phone to get a picture but it sees me coming and flies off strongly.

This, I would go on to discover, is typical. The reference book described them as being abundant in the right place: sheltered damp grasslands. The grass of the moorland meets the shelter of the scrub-lined track and suddenly there are Scotch arguses everywhere, males every few metres flying in search of the slightly more dully marked females, feeding on the profusion of thistles along the old bank. It is thrilling – these are the sort of numbers that I thought were consigned to the history books, a last natural hurrah.

It feels bewildering, this sheer abundance of the Scotch argus. It's almost a sort of vertigo of expectation, to go from a handful to over a hundred in the space of a week.

But even here, this wild moorland that thrums with arguses, is not free from our insidious effects.

The Scotch argus is on the edge of its range. In Britain it is, as the name indicates, a Scottish speciality: there are only two remaining English colonies, but the species has wider horizons and can be found across the mountainous areas of Europe. It is one of the links that joins the Swiss Alps and the rolling moors of Galloway. The genus, *Erebia*, is found across the entire northern hemisphere. The family loves the harsher, colder climate. It is plentiful in the right places for now but the future is ominous.

The need for cold is something it shares with the mountain ringlet, the most upland of British butterflies and another species that links the Swiss Alps and the Lake District fells or the West Highland Munros. The mountain ringlet isn't as abundant as the Scotch argus though. Whereas the distribution map of the argus has moved north by 70–100 km in the past two decades in response to the warming climate,[11] the mountain ringlet cannot follow suit. Its delicate wings, with markings like a smudged Scotch argus, aren't used to big flights. Instead they are moving upwards. Over the same period, they have gone higher in the hills by 150 metres. This might not sound much, but they are found between 400 and 750 metres above sea level already. There's not a lot more ground for them to move up to. Even here, these wild places are not refuges from our cooking of the climate. What we experienced today was an exceptional summer's day. And it feels bleak to think about it – like the memento mori in old paintings of Arcadia – that too many days like these have a counterpunch. They are a sort of debt: if we are not careful, we will pay for them with the lives of our specialist butterflies.

Summer nights: the desire is to sit out, enjoying the warmth that the languorous hours hold as the light slips out of the sky, draining the colour of the day, as the moths replace the butterflies and orbit the street lights in a buzz of confusion.

The nights here have become dark again (the dark returns so quickly after the solstice high); while I'm stuck doing the nightly washing up, the kitchen light attracts multiple large yellow underwings, fluttering against the glass, flashing their normally hidden gold-yellow hindwings, legs pawing at the glass as if desperate to get out of the garden and in from the dark.

Nocturnal creatures are obscure. They are hard to find, identify and monitor. Insects are even more elusive, and where even nocturnal birds have long data sets and wide public concern, for moths it's not the same, not when there's normally a pane of glass between the observer and the observed.

Butterfly Conservation's most recent report into the state of Britain's moths reveals a divergence between abundance and distribution. It found, in the long-term trends that it could calculate, that marginally more species (187 to 165) had increased in distribution rather than decreased.[12] On the flipside, four times as many moths had decreased in abundance than increased. There is an overriding sense of nature being stretched and stressed, smaller numbers pulled over a wider area. Fluctuations in populations are not simple stories, not two-dimensional pictures.

The world is getting warmer. This is no surprise. But nights are getting warmer more quickly than days are, and it is caused by clouds. This is one of the earth's incredible intricacies, the sort that sometimes boggles my brain to try even to think about in its entirety, yet this one can be explained with staggering ease. Clouds insulate. They diffuse the influence of the sun, lessening it, suppressing the daytime's temperature rise. But, at night, those clouds insulate, stopping the earth's warmth from escaping.[13] The scientists who discovered this went on to find the effects of the night warming went hand in hand with greater levels of rainfall and humidity, lessened photosynthesis and worsened conditions for plants to grow in.[14] Moths and butterflies feed on plant nectar, as well as laying their eggs on certain species, for their caterpillars to feed on. Warming nights are counter-intuitively bad for moths to fly around in, for butterflies to breed in.

The future remains hard to call. Butterflies and moths are so culturally associated with hot, dry summers that it seems logical that they would be doing OK. And some are: red admirals seem well set. But then so does the oak processionary. We know that butterflies are capable of staggering acts of adaptation, like the comma switching food plants, and turning from specialist to generalist. We know that we are poised to receive more species from southern Europe that seem to be flying across the English Channel more frequently than before. The risk is distraction, that if we take our eye off the mountain ringlet and Scotch argus while we marvel at the Jersey tiger, when we look back they might have vanished.

Soprano Pipistrelle

It is an odd sensation to meet a roosting bat, upside down and not wavering across the sky at dusk. It takes a second to read it properly. Those aren't hands but feet, its five toes curling into the wall, gripping, like a tiny human hand. Its chocolate-coloured, soft-looking fur body is bordered by the biggest wing bones, seemingly shrink-wrapped in the leather-like skin of the folded-in wing. Further down the wing bone, a hooked thumb extends out at the bottom to anchor it to the wall. Its head is down as if shy, its ears like the tailfins of a squat spaceship, tapering to the point of its nose.

It was odder still to have been stopped by a group of children behind the Robert Burns Centre, who want to know what they should do with it. But neither of us knows much about bats. We convince them to stop poking it with a stick. That's all we know to do. We carry on, heading home at 9 p.m. on a light July evening, the sky clear and cloudless. It is still the best part of an hour before sunset. We get home, change into pyjamas, put our feet up, exhausted by the long walk.

And then we think about the bat.

And the Bat Conservation Trust's website gives us a dreadful sinking feeling. It is clear that a bat in the open in the daytime needs help.

We are back out the door in minutes, clothes thrown back on over pyjamas, and I'm holding a shoebox with airholes skewered into it, a tea towel and a pair of gloves.

As animal house guests go, a bat is a dream. It doesn't make any noise. It doesn't knock over the milk bottle cap filled with water that we give it, nor does it freak out Morag (our cat), as a rescued baby gull had loudly done last summer. In the morning, we check on it just once to make sure it has survived. It has crawled into a comfortable position, nestled in the towel. When Lisa, the local volunteer bat rescuer, comes later that morning, it's almost a shame to have to part with it. Dreams of life as bat carers flash across our minds.

It's perhaps not exactly true to say that I know nothing about bats. I had already seen a bat in trouble earlier this year. I was leaving the car park at Caerlaverock when I looked up. Inky dusk. Flickering shape. A small bat – a pipistrelle – jinking through the darkness in the middle of winter.

I knew enough then to know it was wrong. Bats hibernate, descending into a winter torpor, living off the layer of fat they produce over the summer from eating up to 3,000 insects a night.[1] There are not 3,000 insects in the night at Caerlaverock in January, when it's cold enough to require I wear my fleece indoors. Sleepless winters are not good news for our summer wildlife. But there was nothing I could do for that one.

During the week we get updates about the bat by text. He's a soprano pipistrelle and five weeks old, Lisa reckons, speculating that the stormy night before we took him in had probably disorientated the bat, too young to handle the unseasonal weather. She sends us a picture, the pipistrelle sprawled on a pale blanket, two mealworms in its mouth.

A week later we turn up in the park at 9.30 p.m. to see it released. Lisa produces a clear Perspex box and a heat pad for it to sit on – warmth to rouse the pipistrelle, to make it active. The sky is pale blue, turning gold at the edges. When the gulls flock over the river, they're caught in the golden light. The birds are not a brilliant sign for a bat release and nor is the light evening, Lisa explains. Gulls, omnivorous, would see a bat held out for release as nothing more than a snack.

We don't want that to happen. The bat stays in its box. We wait.

Nice July days in Dumfries have long evenings, but when the light slips away, it slips fast. Reasonable daylight fades to the indigo night with the jolt of a surprise. One moment you are watching birds and the next there is nothing and the dull static of the bat detector begins to twitch.

Lisa lifts the pipistrelle out. It scrambles down her arm. She picks the bat up again, holds it once more. Sitting on her hand, it seems to have a mouse-like body shape – pointy nosed and bulbous at the back end. Its nose curves up into a flat face, and its small triangular ears stand up and out, equal in height to its hindquarters. I have never seen a bat like this before, never had the privilege of this angle in this light.

Then it begins to quiver its wings. Its body vibrating, warming up, easing life back into its minuscule muscles. It reminds me of a moth, but then it flicks a wing out and it is nothing like a moth: its body possibly the width of three fingers in size, but a single wing covers Lisa's gloved palm. It is as though it has undergone a complete transformation, as if it is an entirely different thing from what we found on the wall.

And then the pipistrelle leaps off – our hearts in our mouths – and gently falls like a paper dart, a smooth landing in the park grass. It is an awkward time: no longer new to life but new to flying, its four nights in a box comprising a substantial percentage of the time during which it should have learned to fly. Lisa picks it up again and holds it up once more. Evidently the life of a volunteer bat carer is one of utmost patience.

It is 10.20 p.m. The night is 9 degrees and a chill is setting into my underprepared bones. I take the bat's lead, fidgeting to warm up.

The bat detector's percussion speeds up. In the vestigial light we can just about make out the pipistrelle's mouth moving. It is calling, calls we can lipread but hear only in translation. Suddenly the other soprano pipistrelles have descended from the treetops and are swirling, swooping around the bat in Lisa's hand. The detector goes haywire with noise. Our faces feel the backdraft from batwings.

'They're talking to it,' Lisa says. 'Short of picking it up, there's not much more encouragement they can give.'

Half past ten. Night now. The pipistrelle has remembered how its wings work, what species it is and what it does. And it leaves without fanfare. It just detaches itself from Lisa's raised hand and disappears into the night.

The buzz we get is deep, the warmth of joy and relief spreading through our cold bodies, our cold bones. I feel emotional, for one small life given another chance. And we all – human and bat – head our separate ways into the night.

8

The Illusion of Wildness

I like peat. I like peat underfoot, soft to the step and slightly trembling, the land viscous with it. I like what peat does to water, the way it darkens the depths but gives it a glossy reflectiveness. In the calm of this morning, Knowetop Loch is held still, a black loch with a green paisley of lily pads; a dark mirror for the pine trees on the far bank, where an unseen red kite is keening. I had been needing this.

After our July of recalibration, it feels good to get out. In this summer of reduced horizons, to be the only person on the path, in the wilderness that lies close to home, is lighting my mind with an indelible joy: all the details feel important. The bog asphodel, growing as golden hands reaching up to the blue sky; the heather flowers turning pink; mushrooms lemon yellow in the shade of the floor; the orange and brown of the Scotch argus that flits through the long grass like a piece of peat, scuffed up from the path but suddenly light enough to land in the grass stems without bending them. A flock of swallows flickers over the loch, parting the still dark surface by drinking while on the wing, then veering up, plucking unseen insects out of the air. All of this – almost viscerally needed. While I had spent most of lockdown wanting to see my family and friends, the pull of being outdoors, alone, still trumps everything.

After recalibration comes reparation. Some months change like the flicking of a switch and the cold, wet disappointment of July has given way to the payback of August. Today is creeping above 20 degrees by late morning: this feels exceptional.

The wild is subjective and hard to define. But it's important for me to be somewhere open, somewhere our physical influence recedes and the lives of other species play a bigger role; to feel as if I am in a place that is shared, not dominated. It's good for us and good for everything else here, even if this seems harder every year.

I turn away from the loch and walk the moorland path, fringed with heather and long grasses, while the peat underfoot shows the effect of the wet July. There is a stretch of boardwalk here – over one indistinguishably wetter bit – where I find what I'm looking for: a series of small dark flittings through the wet heather, like glitches in my vision.

They are not glitches. They are black darter dragonflies, basking on the grey wood of the boardwalk, gluttons for this heat. The males black-bodied and black-eyed, interrupted only by faint yellow-brown markings on the side of the thorax and a light-brown down of hair. The females are a dirty yellow, the colour of parched summer grasses, with delicate black lines marking out the edges of their segmented bodies. They are our smallest species of dragonfly, as wild and electric as they all are, charged by the trembling of foot on boardwalk, flitting up and off and landing a few metres further back with every step.

I had waited all summer for it finally to be acceptable to visit the local uplands, the hills to the west of the town that hide the setting sun every evening. I wanted to see and feel this unfamiliar habitat, its unfamiliar life to this native lowlander. Most of Dumfries and Galloway, away from the Solway hinterland, is upland without ever ascending to particularly dramatic heights. It's open to interpretation, to the subjectively drawn boundary between lowland and upland. I draw it with these darters. Black and common darter are species of late summer: they both hang on, making the most of the warmth, extending the season as far as it will go. The difference is where they do it. Common darter I'm deeply familiar with, at sea level, in hedges, woods, marshes – although they can occasionally be found at altitude. The black darter, a species new to me today, can be found in Galloway at sea level or at 500 metres, but it prefers somewhere in between, needing the acidic boggy pools of the peatlands.[1]

There's magic in these uplands – between moor, loch, rock and forest. The spell works best when it's unexpected, stumbled across by accident, where you bring no preconceived ideas and the wild heart of it is revealed with each step. Galloway describes itself as the forgotten corner of Scotland but it wasn't always so. Memories linger in the megaliths and carved stones marked out on the map, in the independent streak that remained after the area was taken over by Scotland in the thirteenth century and survived the population's slow retreat from the rural to the city.

We head back to the track where we found so many Scotch argus before. The walk begins not so wild: ruler-straight, along an embankment that bridges rough ground. But we are barely a few steps down the embankment when it dawns on me that this is a special place. It starts with the wild flowers that I recognise: the lesser stitchwort and the harebells, the St John's wort, toadflax and lady's bedstraw. I am no botanist, and I'm pleased to be able to name twenty-four species before I reach the ones whose multiplicity escapes me: thistles, various; umbellifers, several; the vetch with the name that I once knew but currently escapes me. In a trackside tree, the cartoon tooting of a nuthatch is noisy in the quiet morning. Overhead an *Accipiter* hawk exits the forest, the pursuer noisily pursued by swallows.

This embankment is an old railway track, shuttered since 1965 by Dr Beeching's erasure of our rail network. In the absence of trains, with the track taken up, nature has taken over. Galloway might now be ignored, passed over by people in search of the border hills or the Highland glamour, not willing to venture this far away from the fast roads, yet it was here, on this old railway line, that Richard Hannay flees in John Buchan's *The Thirty-Nine Steps*: 'I fixed on Galloway as the best place to go. It was the nearest wild part of Scotland . . . not over thick with population.'[2] Some things don't change, but Beeching has made following Hannay's escape impossible. It was not his intent to give us this rewilded walking track but that is what he did. By removing the disturbance of trains groaning up the hill, this corridor of space was opened up, a place of difference to the bog or forested spaces around them. Nature abhors a vacuum. Or perhaps it's a case of give nature an inch and it'll colonise these miles, repurposing the land for its needs – a self-made reserve.

We enter the shade of the timber plantation, the track incised deep into the rock, the steep walls of the cutting green with moss and wild strawberry leaves, the air heavy with the scent of pine and bracken. It smells wilder than it is; the trees are planted with regimental organisation, well surveyed and kept for the purpose of making money and product. No light penetrates their depth. An old wall in the wood has crumbled into a pile of stones.

This is not wilderness but there is wildness where the trees haven't smothered all other life. A froglet hops out from the side of the track, where the ditch runs with clear, cold water. Wild raspberry grows and a dead man's fingers fungus has come up at the side of the track, pallid and bending slightly, as if grasping at the world above ground. The pines open up at Loch Stroan, where the track crosses on an old viaduct. The loch water is a perfect, still, blue reflection of the sky. The edges are messy with rushes, beaten back in parts by sunbathers.

This is not wilderness and it feels important to make the distinction. Wilderness is an impossibility in modern Galloway and modern tamed Britain where we tidy it on to nature reserves, but the wild is always there. Wilderness is the non-human; it precludes us. Whereas wildness – that tangible riot of unconstrained life – colonised this man-made habitat, this line cut through forest and moor along which trains used to hurtle. Wildness gives us the rush-edged loch and the wild-flower-spangled banks. This is what is important. And here, on this hot day, it is stunning.

We keep walking with no further purpose, punch-drunk on the pleasure of the day, the delight of plentiful life, the wildness with its myriad butterflies, dragonflies, stonechats calling from the highest of the heathery patches and families of meadow pipits trailing ahead of us. A few miles later the track skirts a further loch, Loch Skerrow, where there is a halt, where steam trains would take on water, pumped from the loch. Two platforms remain, the concrete decaying, green with grass and yellow with lichen. The water stills runs through the culvert, but it is only water mint that drinks there now. In the bracken, broken rusting metal and old concrete of more indeterminate uses. Towards the loch, a flock of several hundred swallows are flitting, glistening as the light sparkles on the water. In keeping with the mood, the strange air of the place, the swallow flock pauses briefly in the tops of a few small pines, like strange bunting. Thistles grow in a profusion between the concrete: Scotch arguses stop their flight at each one, pausing like passengers changing trains, rushing to the platforms of new thistles.

We walk back, more slowly, sated by the abundant butterflies and sun. The day's heat peaks at 27 degrees, the overhead sun now reaching down into the cutting, erasing shade.

We leave the track to cut down to the bank of Loch Stroan, the forest hiding the view until you turn a bend and the loch – azure, sparkling on this sweltering summer's day – is revealed as some Nirvana through the parting pine curtain. Miranda throws herself into the loch – a brief world of sapphire – and floats as if it's the Mediterranean Sea, and I, being non-amphibious, bask as if this rock were a beach. Weed in the water ripples with the flow, green lines in the black water. Rushes by the bank splay green lines in the opposite direction, and a green leafhopper, a strange insect that bears a resemblance to a shrunken, misshapen grasshopper, bounces on a rock. And that's where I'm looking at when the dragonfly zips past my ear.

A golden-ringed dragonfly. It looks like a wasp on steroids, alternating lines of yellow and black on the thorax, the yellow becoming thin rings on the mostly black abdomen, its size big enough to terrify those taken in by the deception, though it is quick and uncurious as a species. It shoots off for a puddle, pauses and bends its abdomen down, dipping the tip in the water repeatedly, revealing her sex. She does this at speed, looking as if she's bouncing, a one-legged miracle walk on water. She's laying eggs, not in the water but below the water, into the damp soil. When they hatch, the larval stage of the dragonfly is where they earn their name, incessantly hunting, the scourge of small pondlife: the basic anatomy of the body is there but they look flattened, crustacean-like, until they walk out of the water, unzip themselves from their skin and attain their final form: winged, eyed and fully bodied. The golden-ringed can spend five years as larvae, the dragon of the watercourse, a long down payment on the future of this puddle, lying undisturbed, not drying out, its own mini-ecosystem functioning for the next five years.[3]

I can't think about five years yet: I can't think beyond the here and now in this moment. We are woozy with heat, hypnotised by her, even after she slips away, leaving us awed by her transient wild magic.

Picture as little of this as you want. It is the next night. I am in bed, three pages from the end of a novel I have been enjoying. My hand brushes over my gut and feels a little something, scab-like, where there shouldn't be anything.

Under the weak light of the bedside lamp I see a small black dot, surrounded by slightly reddening skin. A sinking feeling. I am paranoid about this. I have two different types of tick-removal tool. I always tuck my trousers into my socks, shirt into belt, whenever I go anywhere with undergrowth or long grass. It's been thirty hours since we left the track; it has survived two showers and I'm baffled about where it's been hiding, this cursed peppercorn-sized arachnid, limbs held out, jaws clamped into my skin.

Neither of my tools quite reach it. I have to wake Miranda up to tweezer the blasted thing out of me.

For the next few days I monitor the area. I got away with it, my skin returning to normal, my nerves taking a little longer: any blemish, speck of dirt, makes my stomach churn before I confirm the lack of limbs and jaws. I live in fear of symptoms but nothing comes.

Ticks are the trouble with the wild. We want that seductive magic but, as in all stories, seductive magic has its downsides. Sometimes we have to pay for it in blood. Ticks are a reminder that I too am a mammal, that I too have a role in a food chain that no amount of supermarket shelves can quite remove us from. For a tick, anything with flesh and blood is a target, a delicious meal. I prefer to ignore the fact that I'm a loose bag of blood and bones – or that in return for sustaining them, they could pass Lyme disease on to me here, Mediterranean spotted fever in Sicily, encephalitis in Russia . . .[4]

The effect is most easily seen in America: in nineteen years, they have noticed a three-week advancement in black-legged tick phenology: that is to say that they're getting a three-week head start on growing from where they used to be.[5] Climate is charging them up: they breed more quickly, their population growing and spreading. By 2100 America is predicted a 92 per cent increase in Lyme-disease cases. And that, the scientists say, is a conservative prediction.[6] The likelihood is something similar happening here, in a country with a rampant deer population, beloved by ticks. We don't know yet whether it will, or if it will be as severe as in America. But the danger lurks; the wild bites back.

The heat held.

Since the third week of July, the fields here have been slowly becoming a patchwork of browns in the horizon's sweep of green: the crops harvested, the grasses turning to seed, the shadow of autumn stretching across the landscape. For Robert Burns, his 'Song Composed in August' begins with westerly winds bringing 'autumn's pleasant weather'.[7] I suspect the climate has changed since then. Last August was unpleasantly autumnal, wet and cold. This August is still, in the middle of the month, thick with summer. We have come upriver. North not west, towards the green heart of what is defiantly old Dumfriesshire, not Galloway, for a change. To travel up the Nith is to travel into the heart of Burns country. But we have come not in search of him, but of that other Scottish perennial, castles.

We have come to Drumlanrig in these last days before the Scottish kids return to school, while the English are still on holiday; we are tourists in our own area. The car park overflows with assorted British accents. It's no surprise: the Scottish uplands would not be what they are without castles. History and power and ownership expressed in brick and stone. They are a way of saying that no matter how wild you think this place may be, it is not half as wild as it once might have been.

Although this wildness was not Drumlanrig's domain. There's a clue to that as you cross the bridge across the Nith: the road changes from standard dark asphalt to red, and as the red road sweeps up through a park of sheep and scattered old trees, it turns to face the castle down a tree-lined avenue that recalls The Mall in central London. The road lines up with the castle beyond: staircase split around cloisters, leading up each side to the main door (recalling, to me, the jaws of a spider's face, windows for eyes, an effect I presume not intended by the architect).

It is a building that exists to demonstrate the ownership of money and land through architecture and material: the castle is built in well-maintained pink sandstone. It is the gaff of the Duke of Buccleuch and Queensberry: the man who owns the second-largest swathe of Scotland. The aesthetic appeal of the castle – as striking a building as it is – is diminished by this for me. Around it are his woods, where I'm happier to walk, the way traced along the Marr Burn, looking for Andy Goldsworthy's sculpture of an arch in the water, modelled on the wild upstream leapings of a salmon.

Down in the woods, I notice a skeleton. A few brown lines: a spine and ribs, rough-edged, not quite picked clean. The green solidity of the leaf eaten away. And another leaf: green at the tip only, a handful of wiggling larvae. Sawflies, of some species, wiggling until I look too closely and they freeze, their black heads locked onto the leaf, small green bodies curving along the edge of the leaf, tipped yellow at the end. I lean back. They wiggle wormily back into action, stripping the pathside sapling: the other greener leaves have even larger quantities of larvae on it.

Sawflies eat their greens. They are not a true fly, but a suborder of the Hymenoptera (the grouping of wasps, bees and ants). The name comes from the serrated edge of the females' ovipositor, the appendage they use for cutting into plants and then for laying eggs. They hatch into the larvae, barely a fingernail in length, that are entirely stripping the leaves. *The Very Hungry Caterpillar* has nothing on them.

This unlucky sapling is bearing the brunt of them this summer. It happens: if the larvae remain unnoticed by the birds, they could potentially kill the tree. But it says something else to me. That nature in these wooded slopes remains wild, rebelling in the shadow of the castle and its manicured lawns. Even a duke, who owns the land and the landscape, cannot fully control what happens within it. It said something more extreme to Burns, who, walking near here, imagined the spirit of the Nith telling him about the destruction of the woods. Cankerworm, Burns asks? The Nith tells him that the worm responsible 'wears a ducal crown.'[8]

A short drive down the road is a better castle. Morton Castle is the anti-Drumlanrig. Where one is a monied and manicured pose, the other is contested, a ruin of uncertain, argued-about purpose. It is not down friendly roads. There is no visitor infrastructure beyond a gate, a rough path and a handful of old signs. There is not much here at all but four walls, a crest in the land and a loch. The website Undiscovered Scotland says, 'The truth is that there's actually not all that much to see here beyond the stone walls . . . [but] this really is Undiscovered Scotland and you should come simply to enjoy the location and listen to the wind.'[9] Or as it is now on this still afternoon, the incessant whistling of a young buzzard across the loch, from the top of a tree begging for its parents hanging in the sky above.

Morton is small. A roughly misshapen sort of rectangle. We walk around it before entering, admiring the neatness of the stone walls, in a better state than most buildings half its age. We step up a temporary staircase made of planks and scaffolding. We find Victorian graffiti inside: a wooden door floridly etched with a pair of names, dated 1881. We look down into the castle's pit prison, imagining being consigned to its fetid depths.

'Oh!' we say in sync when a frog moves.

Except we describe different frogs. We are looking in different places. After they acclimatise to our presence on the skyline, they all begin to creep through the fallen bird nests, the black slime and green moss of the castle's damp depths. We count twelve brown frogs: some huge, fist-sized, shuffling through the darkness on bulging limbs; two toads, squatter and rounder, their drier skin darker, not gleaming with the light; and a smooth newt, slight and thin and darkest of all, scampering a slalom around the frogs. And this feels better than the sawflies of the Drumlanrig woods: this is not the rebellion of wildlife but wildlife taking over. Our structures repeatedly become theirs.

We emerge from the castle's dark, back into the bright of this hot afternoon. Damselflies – azure and emerald – flit in the long grass. Swallows and sand martins take their scything flights over the surface of the loch. The path runs around it and heads up through some woodland on the other side. We don't take it, distracted by thoughts of ice cream in the town that the map says is two miles below us but that feels as if it exists in a different world. There's a different world ahead of us too: beyond the wood, a bank of hills that more than doubles our height above sea level. The heather and grass bright but not yet in peak bloom, the cover of vegetation fraying slightly, pulled too thin over the granite scree. The classic uplands.

The hills look good. The hills beckon.

The penultimate day of the month. We wake to the windows fogged up with condensation, the dew sparkling on the grass. The sun has lost its warmth and there's a scent – barely there but perceptible – of autumn on the air. We head for those hills.

Wanlockhead gets its name from the Gaelic 'Cuingealach', meaning 'narrow pass'. It makes sense. Turning off the fast road north from Dumfries at Mennock, you enter the pass. Or rather, squeeze into it, the car threading around sharp bends and through a wood for the moment still green. Then the wood fades away; the car rumbles over a cattle grid and the name explains itself. The expected view of open hills isn't there; instead all we see is a tight valley, the width of the road, river and a sheep-grazed verge, wide enough for a handful of campers. The steep sides are red with heather and striped with scree the colour and weight of rainclouds. It is stunning but that sensation tips over into something else, something I wasn't expecting. The road ahead kinks between the outstretched limbs of hills. It disappears from sight. And I feel briefly claustrophobic, sandwiched by 100-metre-high walls of rock each side, closer than expected. Most of the feeling passes quickly. As the road ascends up the northern side, the valley widens by a fraction, the car pointing towards the sky, ears popping, jaws slack at the view until we arrive at the peak of the pass. Here, 467 metres above sea level, is the village of Wanlockhead: Scotland's highest.

It is an improbable place for a village, sitting in a three-way junction of valleys, surrounded by moorland, heather and grass, and clear-running burns. The reason for it is not immediately clear. A little of the claustrophobia of the pass lingers. The hills seem to press in at the sides of the village that submits itself to the folds of the landscape.

We have no plan. This trip out was a spur-of-the-afternoon-forecast one: 12 degrees but dry with no wind. Good enough.*

As we leave the village, the valley opens up: the lush grass glows emerald when the sun breaks through the moving clouds. Red splashes of heather, olive blankets of sphagnum moss, bright green hummocks of star moss that I can't resist dipping my fingers into, for it holds more warmth than the air does today. A bend in the valley reveals a slag heap piled high, in a shape similar to Suilven, or a dune of detritus. There's gold in these hills. Silver, zinc and copper too.[10] But Wanlockhead was built for lead. It lived for lead. And what remains: a hillside shattered open. The piles of rubble. A beam engine sunk into the ground, like a mutant seesaw. Some preserved miner's cottages and the shattered

---

* More than good enough for here. A mile down the road is Leadhills, Scotland's second highest village, where the average daily temperature is 6 degrees.

exuviae of buildings no longer required, the insides cast away, the roof and high walls sloughed off.

This is the post-industrial uplands. A valley worked and then laid to rest, abandoned to sheep and rabbits and the meadow pipits moving from field to fence as families. We head halfway up the nearest grassy slope, bending back around the flank of a hill before we stop. This is not the right direction. Not what I was looking for. I don't want history today; I want the now. (I am unpopular for this.)

We take the Southern Upland Way south out of the village as it heads up Lowther Hill, beyond the grazed fields, past the rabbit-and-sheep-shit-strewn path. We head higher, into the heather. The path is steep. A pause to catch our breath lets the midges catch us: we are driven on, driven up, arms flailing at the minuscule flies that are honing in on the corners of our eyes, ear lobes, nose tip.

This hillside is not quite the post-industrial upland of the other valley. The track through the heather switches back, crosses a small burn on a good wooden bridge and leads up to a road. Ahead, on the green sweep of the summit of Lowther Hill, is a radar station: a dull white sphere on a narrow base. The shape reminds me of the Google Maps pin, which makes a sort of sense. Its job is tracking the locations of passing air traffic. This hill is connected to the sky, communicating with the unseen, fixing places, while I trace my finger along the orange contours of an OS map, trying to work out how high up we are, while midges remind me exactly where I am and what I am. There might now be the battered patchwork tarmac of a service road under my feet, but I am still 600 metres up: as high as we've been all summer, and on the border between Dumfries and Galloway and South Lanarkshire. And whether it's height or the contours of the hills and the stillness of the air, we have temporarily found silence. A wheatear watches me from a snow pole by the road's edge. Meadow pipits scurry under a crash barrier. A raven breaks the spell, calling from high up and I see a loose line of five, all flying along the hill line. A buzzard slips below us along a patch of dark, burnt heather, blending into the darkness.

Ahead: the high grey clouds end just above distant western hills, a splash of apricot light over the dark hills of Carsphairn and Scaur, the black plantation forestry and the pea-green cow fields that glow when the sun breaks through the clouds in the middle distance. The Mennock Pass can't be seen from here, the narrow valley road swallowed between smooth-sided hills in a trick of the landscape. The contours are smooth but the surface is not: straggly moor grass, heather blooming or burnt scree fields form a ragged quilt of upland colours – grey, maroon and green. To the east the Lowthers roll gently into brown grass moor that seems without end until grey horizon. Northwards: waves of smaller hills, crested with heather, plantation forest, wind turbines until grey space, the same colour of haze as the horizon to the east. But it's not the limit to what we can see. Yesterday we were at the coast and could see down the Solway to the Isle of Man with a clarity that belied the fifty-mile distance. Today we can see further: beyond Glasgow to granite perfection; the jagged triangular Bens of the West Highlands.

Distance does things to me. These days are as if blessed by an atmosphere of crystal clarity, a sensation I associate with winter, not August. I keep a mental list of massive views I have seen, with a slight compulsion towards bigger; my mind likes to be reminded of my incredible smallness and insignificance in the vastness of the world. It was just a short way northeast of here and a month later that Hugh MacDiarmid would have rested on a hillside like this and seen the view that inspired a section of one of his long poems, *Direadh*, which has become famous and is frequently anthologised as a poem in its own right. 'Scotland Small?' finds the poet nestling in a heather hillside, addressing the question of Scotland's status as a nation in its hillside flora while surrounded by many of the species we have seen today (tormentil, harebell, sphagnum, rowans). He finds the importance in the micro – the wild underfoot that serves his political purpose. That descent into details opens up the same vertiginous scale that I get from tracing the horizon to its furthest extent. But whichever way you look, up or down, it does not matter – we would agree on these points: Scotland is closer in size to the infinite than the small and these hillsides are the gateway to that understanding. All it takes is looking.

But let me trace some other details that MacDiarmid would also agree with me about. If Drumlanrig is a building designed to project wealth, then these are hills managed to perpetuate it. As we descend through the heather, we experience it just beyond a burnt patch. A chuck-chuck-chuckling sound. I reply: 'go-back-go-back-go-back' and three red grouse fly in, on a short burst of wingbeats, powering portly bodies with maximum effort. They land in the heather, disappearing: maroon on maroon. Then heads pop up, each bearing a bright red comb arched like a suspicious eyebrow. They bob and walk and bob and cluck, each one personably. It is a gamebird that moves in charismatic ways, that doesn't have the oblivious-to-the-world apparent idiocy of the partridges and pheasants that are bred and released to die; though that too will come to the grouse, soon. August is ending and since the 12th it has been legal to shoot them. Parties of people prepared to shell out the serious money that this takes will be out here doing it.

It's not just this place but hillsides all over the country that are like this. Where the illusion of nature is strong, where it operates on the idea of 'nothing but heather'. This is not a post-industrial upland at all, but one thick in the middle of an industry.

This burnt heather we are near is a form of management. The moor here is also owned by the Duke of Buccleuch and Queensberry. The Drumlanrig website describes the Duke's moors as being 'well-maintained by burning' and also 'stringent vermin control'.[11] Vermin is an interesting word: it means a wild animal that poses a threat to something tended, such as game. The area around Wanlockhead, as the depressing website Raptor Persecution Scotland makes clear, has seen the illegal shooting of a golden eagle[12] and hen harrier,[13] birds that could be seen as vermin by the managers of grouse moors who rely on the removal of predators to keep the grouse populations plentiful. It comes in for visceral criticism on social media.

Much that we think of as new isn't. Criticism of game-keeping practices feels like a recent thing on the internet, yet I have a book, John H. Salter's *Bird Life Throughout the Year*, from 1917, where the September chapter has a subtitle: 'The Sacrifice to Game'. Incidents of herons and hedgehogs killed for spurious game-preservation reasons are detailed. Salter goes so far as to say that these 'are the ordinary victims which constitute the holocaust, the great sacrifice at the altar of game preserving'.[14] He goes on to suggest that illegal pole traps are still used, the law not enforced. This is current today, a century on: a glance at the internet will find instances where pole traps have still been used to kill and injure birds, normally raptors. This might make you think Salter is a surprisingly modern voice – it surprised me to read it – and yet his defence of the kestrel and the merlin's right to life is undercut by an insistence that 'the sparrow-hawk deserves no mercy'.[15]

Salter's conclusion is that with more humanity and nuance, gamekeeping could create a landscape that naturalists would be proud of – a position that nowadays would manage to offend everyone. But at least Salter has argued it: Hamlin's September chapter of *Our Birds Month by Month* touches on birds of prey and the wish that 'their nests escape the ravages of unscrupulous egg collectors . . . the worst enemies of our rarer birds!'[16] Hamlin might as well be a politician offering his 'hopes and prayers' in response to a crisis.

But I digress. The burnt-heather management is carbon intensive. Peat holds carbon. Our uplands hold a lot of it: one of the few things Friends of the Earth Scotland and the Moorland Association can agree on is that there's more carbon held in Scotland's moors than in British woodlands. Burning releases it and other pollutants into the air. The point is to stimulate fresh growth of heather, the shoots of which are particularly nutritious grouse food.

There is little in the way of other vegetation that you might expect to find in the uplands. Heather regenerates better than anything else after fire. These moorlands are tended and manicured by fire, as controlled as any suburban garden.

And I am reminded, as the path makes its final descent back to Wanlockhead, of one of the bitter truths of walking in the countryside: that aesthetics and ecology are often opposed. But there's a consolation here. F. Scott Fitzgerald wrote about the mind's ability to 'hold two opposed ideas . . . at the same time, and still retain the ability to function'[17] and this is useful to contemplate while looking at these heather and grass uplands, and finding them beautiful (as I do) and also devoid of much potential for life (which I also do). Because to walk through them is to submit to miles and miles of just heather. If it wasn't for the aesthetics, it would be hard to cope with. But as I acknowledge this, I also need to acknowledge that almost all the birds I found were around the service track to the radar station, in the interruption to the ocean of heather.

It is a bitter truth I have found repeated all season. This summer has been a time of overwhelming beauty and bleak despair. Some things have worked as they should, while others have fallen apart. Many events have felt deeply unreal and strange, and nature, even though I have found examples of it to be seriously troubling, has provided great relief. So it seems appropriate here, in the crystalline light of the Southern Uplands, as August draws to a close, taking summer with it, that it should be an afternoon in the illusion of nature to bring this into focus.

Wasp Spider

We dropped back down the country. Another week with family before my job starts up again and a reminder of a more familiar August: the sun bright but the morning cool, the swirling breeze sweeping through the house from the open door. The sensation is one of autumn creeping in, tangible but transient. By the late morning we have driven a short distance down the road, parked up and walked back into summer, heat radiating from bare ground, brown grasses wavering in the wind, a speckling of the hardy yellow flowers that have somehow survived. Yet autumn is here too. It doesn't feel like it but I can see it in the fluffy clouds, the sky a deeper shade of blue than at midsummer. I can smell it in the windfall crab apples on the track, crushed underfoot and filling the air with the sweet-sour tang of cider, while the blackberries are beginning to fur up with mould. I can know it in the darter dragonflies – ruddy and common – perched on the bramble leaves, turning as red as an autumn maple until they burn out, the last of summer's insects.

We are walking slowly, searching, our heads hanging low, eyes gazing down, just beyond our shuffling feet. We are searching for spiders. I saw a post on Instagram last year and I had a hunch that this was the place. It's supposedly a heath but it is not a heath that I would recognise by the name, just a couple of dry, long grassy fields spared by the quarry that devoured the neighbouring fields. It is a quiet place, with the wind in the right direction, silencing the quarry and the turning lorries that we can see by the far corner of the field.

The wasp spider is a spectacular species, more dramatic than its chosen surroundings. It is one that I have seen before in the garden of a gite in the heart of France. I was watching a clouded yellow butterfly – an exciting migratory species, sunflower yellow, fringed with black – when I saw it fly into a huge spider's web. The spider pounced, working quickly, trussing up the clouded yellow, the eight points of its feet settling either side of the butterfly, two thick yellow lines on the spider's underside. I was amazed at the speed and size of it: the bold yellow and black stripes were hard to ignore.

This summer is its ninety-eighth in England since its first sighting, a one-off in Rye, presumed to be an accidental stowaway on board a boat. It took until 1940 to be rediscovered here, in a colony in Hampshire, stemming from individuals released after a study in the 1930s.[1] They began the long crawl north, all the way from Hampshire to Bedfordshire. To drive it today would be 118 miles. Now they've made it as far north as the Norfolk coast.

They are a Mediterranean species, marching out of their own accord. They began in the 1950s with the colonisation of Austria, reaching Norway by 2000. A study identified higher average temperatures as the reason for their expansion. The warming summer allows them to spread; the winter temperature holds them back.[2] This hot year should have suited them perfectly.

Searching both sides of the path leads to a sort of dizziness: stems and gaps, grass and space, close and several feet away, a sort of small-scale vertigo, neck ache and grass blindness. And then suddenly it's there, in my vision. A big web with a zigzag* and a big spider suspended in the middle of it. I put my arm up, waving to Miranda, not daring to take my eye off it in case I lose it.

It is not ideal. We have spent an hour walking slowly about these fields and finally we have found one. Miranda's first. I have been hyping the species up, to make this slow, strange walk seem worthwhile. The web is side-on to the path, slanting slightly away, against the light. The spider, fixed in the middle of its web, is sideways on to us, which is the worst angle for seeing a spider. It takes a bit of leaning in to be able to look properly, to see its horizontal wasp-like barring against the stripes of vertical browned grasses, the pale and darker patches on the legs. It's a fine thing. Just . . . underwhelming in the moment.

The second wasp spider is even deeper into the grass, sitting in an even more awkwardly angled web. The third one we find shows the species off. Miranda, competitive, spots it low down, near a bramble – the most obvious of the three – on our walk back; I have managed to walk by it twice without noticing. This one is not underwhelming.

She is facing us, in the middle of its zigzag, the biggest of the day. Her lemon abdomen drawn with inky black lines, some smudgy, some dripping black. Some frame richer yellow lines,

---

* A stabilimentum, characteristic of their webs, a useful detail that helps with finding them.

others circle paler, pithy yellows. Some lines fade out, some are strong. At the front of the abdomen, two small black dots, like an attempt at an extra pair of eyes. The abdomen is oval, almost swollen-looking. She has something trussed up in silk behind her body, a grasshopper I suspect, though it has had the life drained from it to the point of being almost unrecognisable, all limb and deflated skin. Her presence is incredible. They just sit there, bright and bold and take the world on their own terms. They, we agree, transcend the sum of the parts of their name.

All three spiders have been female. The male is a weedy little thing: a quarter of her size, the plain brown colour of grass where the green has been bleached out by the summer-long sun. His entire purpose, his role in life, is to mate. It is the crowning achievement too, for it is normally also the last thing. As they embrace each other, the female trusses him up in silk too. He is protein, after all, not the cause but the fuel for the long walk north.

9

Ghosts of Summer Future

How do you know the season has changed? The transition to autumn seems the slightest of all; detectable in the lengthening of the shadows, the slight slackening in intensity of the heat, the foreshortening of the evenings until they slip away. I had already felt it in the August morning I went looking for wasp spiders but it was just an early hint of what was to come; over a few hours that morning reverted to summer. Now it is mid-September, meteorologically autumn – yet we still seem to be stuck in summer.

Warmth still rules, even now that the evenings are dark, and still visibly declining further. It is another startling underlining of how weird this year has been, from the weather to the wildlife to the pandemic. The virus still lurks, stifling everything, keeping us inside watching the dwindling of light, the curling and dying of leaves, the inverse of when it all began. There is a baffling sensation of a lot having happened, simultaneously with nothing at all – I have seen a lot of wildlife and also not enough. This has just been a snapshot of summer, but also a snapshot of change, as it is happening. And that is something it is important to take note of, while we still can. We must not lose sight of the present while worrying about the future.

We are in Nithsdale, at the back of the Cample Line art gallery, Miranda talking to the staff while I am distracted. We are standing between the gallery and the railway embankment in a shaft of morning sunlight. A chiffchaff sings, a nuthatch toots ebulliently, a goldcrest flits between leaves and a red admiral glides around the top of a tree, small wings held out like sails and for a moment I forget everything. The pandemic is briefly quelled. Things seem OK. And today feels as if it could be a rerun of May, the heatwave May, without the panic and fear of it the first time around. It's amazing what a bit of sun does.

We are here to participate in an art project, walking works of art into the landscape surrounding the gallery. And what a landscape: away from the main road, between the flat valley and the hills, the gallery lies in rolling green, suspended in a lacework of tiny country lanes that fold their way between fields and along burns, sticking to the undulating contours. It's as stunning as anything further into the valley. The verges are thick with stands of willowherb, the fire of its flowers burnt out, turned to the silvery woollen seed heads that curl up at the end like a dandy's moustache. There are fat golden hoverflies sitting on the well-spaced purple spheres of devil's bit scabious. A small tortoiseshell butterfly, recently emerged, feels like a great autumnal luxury, the last hurrah of bold colour that has nothing to do with decay and everything to do with life. We crest a small hill and the Lowthers are revealed in front, the purple patchwork of heather bright under an almost cloudless blue sky, and the hills of Carsphairn to the west, fading out in the heat haze behind a herd of Galloway cattle.

This weather feels as though summer is lingering. Our eyes suggest we are slightly further along: scabious always stays out late in the year, the oaks and beeches that run along the burns and hedges are beginning to turn yellow at the edges, the occasional leaf flutters down and catches my eye, fooling me for a second into lifting my binoculars. Until the real thing appears: a chiffchaff, not a leaf, though you could be forgiven for confusing the two, but it's falling the wrong way, along the branch, rather than down. It slips into song again, a marker of autumn as much as it is of spring, although it isn't known why they sing in autumn.

The temperature is as hot today as anything we've had in the Dumfries summer. Is it an Indian summer? Perhaps it is climate change? Is there any point in trying to tell the two apart? To me this seems to be the underlying problem: navigating our way between weather and climate.

Weather is the raw stuff, the materials out of which a climate is constructed. Observing the weather gives you the data but the noise too. The highly variable climate we have here doesn't help in sifting through the blips, the good days and the bad ones; the good years and the bad ones. But the feeling I have, the feeling that most people I've spoken to share, is that it's been particularly weird this year.

The observatory at Eskdalemuir, the eastern end of Dumfries and Galloway, experienced the wettest February day in its 109-year history: 79.4 mm of rain fell. In the same storm, parts of West Yorkshire received a month's worth of rain in eighteen hours. Later that month, the UK had its second wettest day on record: February became the wettest one since the Met Office began measuring this in 1862.[1] That wet February was followed by the sunniest May, in the sunniest spring on record (by a long way), a swing described as 'unprecedented'.[2] The last day of July was the UK's third hottest day on record (Heathrow reached 37.8 degrees), marking the sixth time the UK's temperature has gone above 36.7 – but the third time it has done so in the last six years.

Summer had one last heatwave: the start of August was the only time in the last sixty years that the UK had six consecutive days of temperatures in excess of 34 degrees. Dumfries then had its lovely September while it rained constantly on England. On 3 October, the UK sets its wettest day on record (of the top twenty wettest days, two occurred in 2020, four more in the last twenty years), and I will remember this as the day I schlepped around town trying to find an anniversary card, failing, and getting completely sodden through all my waterproofs anyway. Such is life, you have to laugh, or you'll . . .

. . . Or you'll cycle back further. To December 2019, when Achfary in Sutherland, the northwest tip of the Highlands, reached 18.7 degrees, the highest December temperature in the UK; in the same year that Kew in February reached 21.2,[3] that the Cambridge Botanic Garden peaked at 38.7 in July. All of these temperature records, in an otherwise sodden year. Or 2018: the joint hottest summer on record, the spring it didn't rain for sixty days where we lived, in Essex, and the grass turned brown and I lived in fear of a stray cigarette or poorly planned barbecue setting the park alight.

The difference between weather and climate is not always clear. But with three years of heat records, anxiety begins to creep up like the mercury of a thermometer on a sunny day. And as I have found this summer, it is impossible not to find the effects – the stresses, depletions, the creeping weirdness of it – throughout the natural world.

I am at work and I get a call from a colleague. They have noticed a caterpillar – huge and green is the description – crawling around by our entrance. It is a poplar hawk-moth caterpillar, its apple-green body quickly shuffling over the black ground, strewn with yellowing leaves from a nearby willow tree. My mind dredges up half-remembered hawkmoth facts: that they pupate underground and that September is late in the year for them to be out.

I cradle it in a large leaf. The poplar is much subtler than the elephant hawkmoth. The colour is lurid but the markings aren't: a small row of indistinct pinkish spots, a series of white diagonal lines, a yellow spike at the back and an upside-down yellow V on the head. I take it to a planter on the patio, where it plays dead on the surface of the soil, pretending to be a lost branch of the fennel that grows here. I give it a few minutes, return and find its head is already under the soil, its body slowly pulsating, digging down until the yellow spike slips away, for its winter underground.

I feel a bit like a parent. I tell my colleagues what's happening and why, and how next year it will emerge as a moth, the size of the palm of their hand, the hindwings held ahead of the forewing in a shape like a partly withered leaf, and how as a moth it won't feed, for it has no proboscis, and has eaten its last meal of willow leaves as a caterpillar. I leave them googling pictures of it as an adult, amazed that such a thing could exist.

The world is still worth taking pleasure in.

It's a lesson I need to keep relearning. I began this year by keeping a list of all the birds that people were seeing in the wrong place. In January I noted down: a turtle dove in a London park, house martins in Sussex, swallows in Essex and a wheatear in County Cork. That was just a handful of days at the beginning of the year. After that the list burned out, my handwriting became illegible, the page in the notebook fell out, floated around my living room for a month before it disappeared under the sofa. I tried to curate a compendium of news articles, opening internet browser tabs to keep track of stories such as the time capsule, buried in ice at the north pole in 2018, that was found this year, the ice having melted, the capsule having drifted the 2,000 miles to the Donegal coast.[4] I was taken by the melancholy of the ephemera: the photographs, badges and beer mats that it contained, too soon to have become memories themselves (the Arctic ice will be a memory sooner).

I gave up shortly after because there was too much: too many things to note, too many small signs of the growing strangeness of everything. I started to recoil from them all. The brain can take only so much bleakness.

Aldo Leopold wrote in *Round River* that 'the penalty of an ecological education is that one lives alone in a world of wounds' and I agree.[5] In response I had grown callused, emotionally, towards the climate; my own adaptation to the diet of bad news we get drip-fed. I don't want that any more.

Earlier this year Miranda wrote a review of a poetry collection. In it she wrote that 'Language is a means of delighting in the world.'[6] She's right – it's part of the reason why I write, to define, expand and explore the delight I feel, the joy of going outside and seeing nature, that I still feel even when confronted by all the evidence of it going wrong.

I am a reformed nihilist about climate change and our declining wildlife. I used to think there was no hope, and that hope anyway is a way of artificially inflating your emotions, that it was better to stare down the barrel of our unrelentingly bleak future. I made a fantastically miserable teenager, as I'm sure you can imagine; a perfect example of a tedious, po-faced environmentalist. The Venn diagram between moral virtuousness and absolute headbanging nihilism overlaps more than you might expect. It was love that changed that. The tenacious sort of love that keeps you outside or looking through a window, permanently on the edge of being distracted by nature. My underlying current of love for wildlife fuels my hope, stops me from recoiling further, away from this wounded world.

It was only recently that I realised this: that I cared too much to continue with my teenage nihilism. That overarching joy I feel about watching nature was always there, and is still present, and will always be there, no matter what. The fascination of watching a blackcap in a gale in Liverpool in January, or a Scotch argus feeding at a moorland flower in Galloway on a sweaty, stifling August day will always override their darker implications. 'We must love', wrote Freud, 'or we grow ill.'[7] I don't want to abandon that love, or the joy and pleasure and beauty of the world, to the worthy and the dreary.

There's an idea – one that comes filed under literary criticism not philosophy, though really it's both – that Timothy Morton writes about, called 'the dark ecology of elegy'. The point of it is that much elegiac writing about the environment 'presupposes the very loss it wants to prevent.'[8] Gloom breeds gloom until that's all you have left, but hope is what is worth holding on to. This does not mean that the loss of wood warblers from our summer woodlands is not worthy of sadness or anger, but the resignation of an elegy is not quite right here. If I were a conservationist, reading an elegy to a species not lost yet, I'd be insulted at the insinuation of my failure. If this book sometimes seems to be filled with misery, it would be good to feel that it's balanced by love and hope. Despite the litanies of wild ghosts; the gone, the going and those to follow after, I'm not yet ready to leave them. Not yet ready to let them die.

A 1995 book called *Birds and Climate Change* asks in its conclusion, 'Do birds and other wildlife play any role in predicting climate change?' The answer is a blunt no – 'but they do provide clear evidence and confirmation that climatic changes are occurring.'[9] That was a quarter of a century ago – a quarter of a century of global inaction and glib political obfuscation ago – and it's still the case. Part of this is the paradox of how we manage to be simultaneously aware of climate change and yet live our lives without responding to it. How we become the ostrich of cliché – head deep in the sand to avoid looking at what's coming.

It is very easy not to think about it at all. It's very easy to do nothing. We all live lives of a certain amount of comfort (or you spend your life trying to attain that comfort) before we focus on other things. Insulated by that, here in Britain, when it is not your crops being ruined, why bother about the climate? Especially if the symptoms of it are more glorious months like this May: a time best spent outside, working on your tan, when all life's problems seem solved by a cold drink in the shade of a tree. Or the roasting August, when we have come to expect the heatwave, the worrying data hidden in plain sight. Or the arrival of more species, exotic novelties from the south, to watch on your local patch – the dazzling diversion of the egrets, foregoing their traditional Mediterranean home to settle on the Somerset Levels, delightful distractions that stop us from thinking about what their presence really means – creeping heat and the loss of those adapted to the cold.

Understanding, comprehending, is hard. Particularly when the detailed science and reams of data mean little to anyone without a science degree. The numbers are the

dreariest of all things to me. Numbers are cold: simultaneously definitive and yet slippery enough to mean anything
at all, as hard to grasp as the carbon dioxide climate statistics describe. The brain does not naturally make sense
of anything reduced to parts-per-million. It's not a human
metric.

I agree with the Indian novelist Amitav Ghosh when
he says that climate change is 'perhaps the most important
question ever to confront culture in the broadest sense . . .
the climate crisis is also a crisis of culture, and thus of the
imagination.'[10]

The realisation that climate is first of all a cultural
problem is quite profound. It gives us a starting point to
work from. It helps us to understand people's attitudes and
reactions – or lack of reaction – to this great untouchable,
intangible, abstract existential threat. It reminds us we have
to take people along with the solution, instead of abandoning them.

There's a great case study in Mary Robinson's *Climate
Justice*: Ken Smith, a worker and union leader, on the oil
sands of Alberta, Canada. Smith had been union president of a mine that closed elsewhere in Canada. The only
employment he could find was working on the notoriously
polluting oil sands on the other side of his country. He spoke
at the Paris Climate Summit in 2015, making the point,
'How are we going to provide for our families? . . . We've
moved out there, invested in the industry – and when it ends
we're going to be left holding the bag.'[11] Wherever you are,

whoever you are, you probably hold more in common with the tar-sands workers than the suits that keep them there.

For too long the focus has been, in the language of Greenpeace Canada, 'defusing the carbon bomb',[12] when the trick is to find a way to transfer people from carbon-intensive, polluting jobs to something that holds the same benefits for them without the environmental cost. People's jobs don't define them, but they can supply a big part of their identity: implying they are a bomb is not helpful, not the way to bring them along.

We must all participate, at every level, in the cultural shift that's needed to make a difference. For the last month an advert on the internet for an energy company has been shouting at me: 'Stopping climate change begins at home.' Because of course the responsibility is ours, and not the inhabitants of stuffy backrooms and boardrooms who wield the actual power to overhaul our financial and political systems. This is what is really needed – structural change at every level; what is not needed is corporations trying to shift their blame onto us, who can choose only from what we're offered, while they continue to operate as normal. It's only by understanding climate properly, culturally, that we can move away from this.

I was cynical as to whether that could ever happen, whether we were capable of such a large-scale cultural shift in attitude. But the pandemic has proved to be an interesting case study in watching us, all of us, adapt to a new way of living, taking a journey from doubt and scepticism to action at the same time. We have proved that we can change our behaviour en masse, particularly with the easy solutions of face masks and hand sanitiser and even the harder things, such as working from home, keeping our distance, being apart from the people we love, the temporary disabling of our social structures. We haven't always kept to them – but we mostly have. At the same time, a small resurgence of interest in nature happened, with people able to hear bird-song after the silencing of our streets. It seemed for some as if nature was healing, when really it was just being given the first chance to shout in half a century. The air felt cleaner, views clearer.

The real question – one I have no possible answer to – is how to keep the changed behaviours. How to make sure that any necessary adaptations we are able to make to address climate change will last, will have the staying power of the face mask and not fall by the wayside like the elbow bump.

The other facet to seeing climate as a cultural problem is that it quietens the voice that's been nagging away in my head. Why am I writing about climate and not doing some-thing more practical, more tangible? Because sometimes cultural problems require thinking, as well as action. I'm not here to tell you what to do. I'm a writer, not a guru. I'm not selling anything except for ideas, not sticking-plaster solutions or salves for your soul (other than suggesting that, if you can, you might like going outside). I write to make these things real.

I am suspicious of philosophy. The writer bell hooks put it brilliantly: 'Any theory that cannot be shared in everyday conversation cannot be used to educate the public.'[13] I agree:

expression is important and so is clarity. The jargon of much of what I read that passes as philosophy seems designed to confuse, to be argued but not believed. Compared to this, wildlife is a beacon of clarity.

One motivation for me spending this long summer writing about wildlife is that I have a belief that ecoliteracy is essential, that it will underpin any successful attempt at saving the world from ourselves. Any writing about wildlife and the landscape is writing about climate too, even tangentially: they are intertwined. Ecoliteracy is being able to see that our changing wildlife cuts through the hot air to the reality of our future. That it is not prediction but reaction.

Ecoliteracy is a neologism – so I should be suspicious of it, as I am with most jargon. But I can't be. Ecoliteracy is not even all that new any more: it's a word that's three months older than I am and it seems to be hanging around. I find it a powerful word: one that goes beyond simply seeing nature and its issues, to being able to understand, interpret and communicate them too. It's recognising how it all fits together; that drought in the Sahel affects the birds of our summer woodlands, that an early spring means early caterpillars, leaving the birds hungry when their young are squawking, naked and blind in the nest. It's understanding the way that these things compound each other.

Everything is deeply intertwined and affected by the climate, and we need to have a better awareness of the life we share our planet with. I think the local is a useful lens to see the wider picture: it offers a starting point, a way to observe and understand nature, to see what we can change and control. To really see what is happening and how it affects us, personally, in our immediate surroundings. In grander reckonings of summer wildlife and the effect of climate, it's species such as the Scotch argus and the azure hawker that get squeezed out of our attention, while we think of the extremes, the egret invasions or knackered polar bears clinging to melting ice.

We've lost the way of thinking locally. Barry Lopez, one of the great American nature writers, believes that 'In forty thousand years of human history, it has only been in the last few hundred years or so that a people could afford to ignore their local geographies as completely as we do and still survive.'[14] He draws that out: fresh fruit all year round eroding the concept of seasons, air travel eroding distance, subsidies for farms leaching chemicals into the environment eroding the idea of responsible stewardship. It would be so easy to keep up this retreat from our surroundings; if the declines in our local patches continue, the sense of loss could become so overbearing that it outweighs the innate joy we take in nature, the simple pleasures of being outside, birding, butterflying, dragonflying. It would be tempting to stop looking, so we no longer have to feel that loss.

Yet now, more than ever, it's important to take notice. In the autumn I read *Weather*, a novel by Jenny Offill. It is a story of the daily life of a woman called Lizzie in New York in 2016, told in fragmentary paragraphs of thoughts. The thoughts string together a web of creeping dread and daily worries: Trump's election, Lizzie's family, the taxi she uses because she's his only customer, the climate. It is perhaps not the ideal thing to read in a global pandemic, but the anxiety seems to tap into the current zeitgeist. One of the story's strands is how Lizzie gradually slips into becoming a doomsday prepper: the logic of not being one unravelling slowly as the worries ratchet up. One of the characters, Sylvia, runs a podcast about the future called 'Hell and High Water' and states, 'There's no hope any-more, only witness.'[15]

I still have hope but I feel the importance of witness-ing more than ever. It's the first of the steps to ecoliteracy. There is no understanding without first noticing, observing, responding. Bearing witness seems a good, hope-filled first step: it suggests a purpose. A defiance to letting this become normal.

You can bear witness to the weather as I have and see its effects in the trees, insects, birds, the things that put the flesh on the bones of a landscape. To notice phenol-ogy, fluctuations in populations and changes in habitat and behaviour. To observe the difference between the hush of summer as the passing quiet of the season and the per-manent silence of absence. The species I've looked at are ciphers: you can replace them with what you have locally, wherever you are. You'll probably notice the same things.

This is what ecoliteracy is: an awareness of what the loss of the Cornish accent from the language of the corn bunt-ing in the hedgerow or the fading away of the azure hawker from a Gallovidian hillside mean, and where those losses fit in the scheme of things. Ecoliteracy is like a good metaphor or a poem in the way it takes something small and particular and applies it to a universal. It's like the slow zooming-out of a camera, from a tiny detail to the whole.

I set out to trace phenology in a year that turned out to have no time. I set out to trace the connections nature gives us in a year that we voluntarily severed connections to save ourselves, when what I thought was local was shifted the best part of 300 miles away. It felt increasingly hard to understand anything at all, a trick our psychology plays on us, inuring ourselves to one existential danger in the face of another, like the pandemic.

I think back to my original wander down the riverside here, that autumn day the year before when the hawthorns were ablaze with berries (they're not this year), when I realised that I could isolate neither warblers from the hedgerow, the hedgerow from the summer, nor the summer from the winter. That vast set of connections, that awe-inspiring web of life that we live in, is still pleasurable; we can still go out and look at it, engage with it, even in its depleted state. But in doing so we must also take note of how it is changing. Nothing I've seen this extraordinary summer – or not seen but meant to – can be isolated from these connections. They seemed so innocent at the beginning, simply showing us how our natural world is intertwined, part of one big, beautiful picture that all seems fine when you look at it from a distance but worryingly fractured when looked at closely.

This is not always obvious either. The Leopold quote I mentioned earlier continues, 'much of the damage inflicted on land is quite invisible to laymen'.[16] I write to make it real. So you'll find me in the forest, by the saltmarsh, up into the heather-clad hills, noticing the signs, bearing witness to the weather and wildlife, locally.

I am not alone in this. Britain's naturalists, the watchers and puzzlers-out of our country's nature, are with me, the witnesses to the future. They give me hope. The birders, dragonfly-lovers, butterfly nerds: responsible for so much of what we know and what we will know of what's going to change in the near future, all underpinned by the same love that drives me forward, not to avert my eyes from nature at its time of need.

And I cannot wait for the next summer, when it is to be hoped that we'll be freer, able to explore nature the way we want to: revelling in the riot of life, not taking the beauty for granted – or ignoring the warnings.

Last Swallow

What does the future of our summers look like? I have no idea; just as I had no idea back in March, when I heard my first chiff-chaff of the year singing, what the year would turn into. We were in the car park of our wedding venue when the chiffchaff charged my mind with the joy of the season to come, while the manager was talking in the subjunctive: 'If the pandemic spares us, if we're still in business.'

It is November now. Summer seems a distant memory. Yet, on the day Miranda and I were due to get married the air is still, the sky blue and the air nips at our ear tips as we walk through Mabie Forest's blaze of beech trees. We come out at a ridgetop and look south to the Lake District, the fells poking through a slight haze over the Solway settling on the Cumbrian coast. It is galling that we got to within three days of our wedding before the second lockdown sealed England off from Scotland, post-poning our future. We walk our sadness off; we eat and drink distraction. It is also galling that it is, according to the forecast, the only nice day this November.

Autumn comes with its days of Indian summer, kidding you into thinking it's still the height of the year, and that time is on your side. But then, undeniably, it changes. October is a lovely month when it's not raining, but when it does it could be deep midwinter. Now, in the last hurrah of November sunshine, the last glimmer of summer in the forecast, we make the most of it, as if we could store it up for what's to come.

We say a final farewell to the summer.

I see a tweet of four swallows lingering in Kent. One swallow doesn't make a summer; it hasn't for two millennia of human existence. Do four swallows, in November, now not mean a winter? Maybe they were a one-off; or maybe this is what the future looks like. Either way, their presence is a reminder of the strange disordering of everything.

I didn't note the departure of swallows from here. I try every year but it just happens, just slips through my fingers: it seems to be data I am incapable of keeping. Like an ebbing tide, by the time you realise something is moving, it is often too far gone. And I am, as I think most people are, inclined to notice presence not absence, the positive not the negative.

I know the redwings have returned – I have heard them calling sibilantly as they migrate at night. I know the skylarks have been moving east through the milky mornings, their calls reaching over the sound of crunching leaves and car engines, their thick wings flickering as they pass as otherwise distant dots. But no fieldfares yet, no whooper swans. It feels like a purgatory, suspended between seasons, beyond autumn but not yet into winter.

And in this seasonal grey area, I find myself yearning for summer again, sorry that it has left – that troubling but shining season of clement weather, when the outdoors is an easier place to hang about and indulge in, when there is time and light.

Those are the first things we lose in autumn, the trigger for the departing birds. But I know the next time I walk down the riverbank, by the hawthorn bushes, daydreaming of warblers, that I'll still find the evidence of summer there, even in the deepest winter.

Acknowledgements

Thanks foremost, always, to family: Miranda (by now, I hope, my wife) and Victoria Cichy, the first readers and untanglers of my first rough sentences. Thanks to George, Suzie and Imran too for putting up with me over lockdown – I hope the bread was worth it. Thanks also to Peter and Elisabeth, my parents, for your unfailing support.

This book was built out of the kindness and conversation of many conservationists and naturalists. Thanks to Stephen Menzie for helping me kick things off on that bleak January day, when we could still enter other people's houses. I'd also like to thank, in particular, Adam Murphy and Andy Over at Dumfries NatureScot for many productive days volunteering on the reserve and my many panicked questions. Thanks too to Brian Morrell and Faith Hillier at the Wildfowl and Wetlands Trust reserve at Caerlaverock, Andrew Bielinski and the staff at RSPB Mersehead and Wood of Cree, and Mark Pollitt at the South West Scotland Environmental Information Centre. You were all very patient with my requests and questions and generous with your time. I must also extend thanks to Steve Blain, Andrew Culshaw, David Howdon, Patrick Laurie, Stephen Moss, and Dr Rob Thomas for their help. As always, any mistakes are mine.

To Lisa Stitt, bat-rescuer extraordinaire, and anyone who works on an animal rescue or information hotline: you are heroes, thank you.

Thanks to my literary sounding boards: David Borthwick, Sally Huband and Richard Smyth. Inspiration doesn't always work in the ways you expect it to; you might not have realised you were helping but you were. So, thank you.

The corncrake section in June first appeared in a slightly different form as a blog post for dgculture.co.uk. Thanks to Fiona for asking me to write it and clarifying my memories, inadvertently fuelling my feelings in the farmland chapter.

Before lockdown, when we used to do literary events in person, instead of online, they had found a way of becoming a sort of shared climate-anxiety therapy session. I found these inspiring, as filled with hope as they were sadness and despair. So thank you to the audience members of any talk that I have done who answered my questions about the signs of change that they had noticed (especially if you were there in Stornoway – that night was magic). To anyone who takes the time to send me a message about the books, or like a social media post, thanks – you help make it worthwhile.

I have long loved the paintings of Daniel Cole and I am delighted that he allowed us to use his art for the cover.

To Elliott & Thompson: especially my editors Sarah Rigby and Pippa Crane for making the book happen, and Jill Burrows for the expert copy-editing. I'd describe you all as indefatigable but you'd probably make me take that out . . .

Notes

Introduction

1. William Shakespeare, Sonnet 18, in *The Norton Anthology of Poetry* (New York: W. W. Norton, 2005), p. 259, l. 4.
2. John Muir, *My First Summer in the Sierra* (Boston: Houghton Mifflin, 1917), p. 157.
3. George Orwell, 'Some Notes on the Common Toad' [1946], in *Spring*, edited by Melissa Harrison (London: Elliott & Thompson, 2016), p. 8.
4. Ibid., p. 9.
5. J. A. Baker, *The Peregrine* (London: Harper Collins, 1967).
6. https://www.ucsusa.org/sites/default/files/attach/2017/11/World%20 Scientists%27%20Warning%20to%20Humanity%201992.pdf.
7. L. P. Hartley, *The Go-Between* (London: Hamish Hamilton, 1954), p. 1.
8. Rachel Carson, *Silent Spring* [1962] (London: Penguin, 2000), p. 22.

Rising Damp

1. Tim Osborn and Douglas Maraun, 'Changing intensity of rainfall over Britain', *Climatic Research Unit Information Sheet No. 15*.
2. https://ueaeprints.uea.ac.uk/id/eprint/74467/1/Dale_Fort_rainfall_ since_1849_accepted_version.pdf.
3. B. Stoker, et al., *Marine Climate Change Impacts Partnership: Report Card 2020* (Lowestoft: MCCIP, 2020), p. 5.
4. https://www.metoffice.gov.uk/weather/climate/climate-and-extreme-weather.

1 Summer in a Blizzard

1. Richard Smyth, *An Indifference of Birds* (Axminster: Uniformbooks, 2020), p. 12.
2. Hadoram Shirihai, et al., *Sylvia Warblers: Identification, Taxonomy and Phyologeny of the Genus Sylvia* (London: Christopher Helm, 2001), p. 35.
3. Ibid., pp. 37–8.

4. D. R. Langslow, 'Movements of Blackcaps ringed in Britain and Ireland', *Bird Study*, vol. 26, no. 4 (1979), p. 248.

5. J. Stafford, 'The Wintering of Blackcaps in the British Isles', *Bird Study*, vol. 3, no. 4 (1956), p. 256.

6. https://www.bto.org/sites/default/files/u23/downloads/pdfs/factsheet_blaca.pdf.

7. Shirihai, et al., p. 37.

8. Tim Birkhead, et al., *Ten Thousand Birds: Ornithology Since Darwin* (New Jersey: Princeton University Press, 2014), p. 65.

9. Jean W. Graber and Richard R. Graber, 'Feeding Rates of Warblers in Spring', *Condor*, vol. 85, p. 139.

10. White, p. 92.

11. Ibid., p. 28.

12. Ibid., pp. 39–40.

13. Glenn Albrecht, '"Solastalgia", A New Concept in Health and Identity', *PAN Philosophy Activism Nature*, no. 3, p. 45.

First Swallow

1. http://classics.mit.edu/Aristotle/nicomachaen.1.i.html.

2 The Lengthening Light

1. Jim Crace, *Harvest* (London: Picador, 2014), p. 19.

2. William Wordsworth, *A Guide Through the District of the Lakes in the North of England (1835)*, Section 89. https://romantic-circles.org/editions/guide_lakes/editions.2020.guide_lakes.1835.html.

3. Ibid., Section 86.

4. Sylvia Townsend Warner, *The Diaries of Sylvia Townsend Warner*, edited by Claire Harman (London: Virago, 1995), p. 132.

5. R. J. Mitchell, P. E. Bellamy, et al., 'Collapsing Foundations: The Ecology of the British Oak, Implications of its Decline and Mitigation Options', *Biological Conservation*, vol. 233 (2019), p. 318.

6. Ruth Mitchell, et al., 'The potential ecological impact of ash dieback in the UK', in *Biodiversity in Woodland Ecosystems*, edited by Glenn Iason (Aberdeen: The James Hutton Institute, 2014), p. 6.

7. Birkhead, et al., *Ten Thousand Birds*, p. 221.

8. Ibid., p. 132.

9. Richard Mabey, *Flora Britannica* (London: Sinclair Stevenson, 1996), p. 262.

10. Flora Thompson, *A Country Calendar and Other Writings* (Oxford: Oxford University Press, 1979), p. 56.

11. http://www.hantsiow-butterflies.org.uk/events/250%20years%20 Hants%20butterflies.pdf.

12. John Berger, 'Meanwhile', in *Landscapes: John Berger on Art*, edited by Tom Overton (London: Verso, 2016), 242–252, p. 246.

Egrets

1. Pete Combridge and Chris Parr, 'Influx of Little Egrets in Britain and Ireland in 1989', *British Birds*, vol. 85 (1992), pp. 16–21.

2. Mark Holling, et al., 'Rare Breeding Birds in the United Kingdom in 2008', *British Birds*, vol. 103 (2010), p. 501.

3. https://www.birdguides.com/news/western-cattle-egret-nests-in-three-new-counties/.

4. B. and R. Mearns, 'The first confirmed breeding of little egret in Scotland, 2020', *Scottish Birds*, vol. 40, no. 4, pp. 305–6.

3 Fractured Rhythms

1. J. A. Baker, *The Peregrine* (New York: New York Review of Books, 2005), p. 151.

2. https://www.bbc.co.uk/news/uk-scotland-south-scotland-22307748.

3. Robert Burns, 'Banks of Cree', *The Works of Robert Burns* (Ware: Wordsworth Editions, 1994), ll. 6–7, 15–16.

4. Margaret Atwood, *The Blind Assassin* (London: Bloomsbury, 2000), p. 395.

5. Malcolm D. Burgess, et al., 'Tritrophic phenological match-mismatch in time and space', *Nature Ecology & Evolution*, vol. 2 (2018), p. 971.

6. T. H. Sparks, et al., *Natural Heritage Trends of Scotland: Phenological Indicators of Climate Change* (Inverness: A Scottish Natural Heritage Commissioned Report, 2006), p. 17.

7. Burgess, et al., pp. 971–2.

8. Wendell Berry, *The Peace of Wild Things* (London: Penguin, 2018).

9. C. T. Agnew and A. Chappell, 'Drought in the Sahel', *GeoJournal*, vol. 48 (1999), p. 299.

10. https://www.aljazeera.com/news/2012/6/22/analysis-understanding-the-sahel-drought.

11. Derek Winstanley, et al., 'Where have all the whitethroats gone?', *Bird Study*, vol. 21, no. 1 (1974), p. 1.

12. Leo Zwarts, et al., *Living on the Edge: Wetlands and Birds in a Changing Sahel* (Zeist: KNNV Publishing, 2010), p. 429.

13. Walt Whitman, 'Song of Myself', *The Penguin Book of American Verse*, edited by Geoffrey Moore (London: Penguin, 2011), Section 51, l. 8.

Dragonflies

1. Alfred Tennyson, 'The Two Voices', *The Poetical Works of Alfred Tennyson* (Boston: Ticknor and Fields, 1860), p. 199, l. 15.
2. Gerard Manley Hopkins, 'As kingfishers catch fire', in *Victorian Poetry: An Annotated Anthology*, edited by Francis O'Gorman (Massachusetts: Blackwell Publishing, 2004), p. 536, l. 1.
3. Steve Brooks and Steve Cham, *Field Guide to the Dragonflies and Damselflies of Great Britain and Ireland* (Oxford: British Wildlife Publishing, 2014), p. 5.

4 Living Landscapes

1. Charles St John, *A Scottish Naturalist* (London: Andre Deutsch, 1982), p. 9.
2. Ibid., p. 76.
3. Ibid., p. 77.
4. Ian Woodward, et al., 'Population estimates of birds in Great Britain and the United Kingdom', *British Birds*, vol. 113 (2020), p. 91.
5. Ibid.
6. Sarah Eglington, 'Understanding the Causes of Declines in Breeding Wetland Bird Numbers in England', BTO Research Report No. 562, British Trust for Ornithology (2009), p. 49.
7. Ibid., p. 51.
8. Stephen Moss, *A Sky Full of Starlings* (London: Aurum Press, 2008), p. 10.
9. Olivia Laing, *To the River* (Edinburgh: Canongate, 2017), p. 258.
10. Ibid., p. 259.
11. See Stephen Rutt, *The Seafarers: A Journey Among Birds* (London: Elliott & Thompson, 2019), p. 2.
12. C. Richard Rutt, *Ash on an Old Man's Sleeve* (unpublished manuscript), p. 21.
13. Ibid., p. 166.
14. Jennifer Smart, 'A question of scale – from nature reserves to landscape-scale conservation', *Wader Study*, vol. 123, no. 2 (2016), p. 83.

Natterjack Toad

1. Trevor Beebee, *Climate Change and British Wildlife* (London: Bloomsbury, 2018), p. 285.
2. https://www.nationalgeographic.com/animals/2019/03/amphibian-apocalypse-frogs-salamanders-worst-chytrid-fungus/.

5 The Reaping

1. Mark Cocker and Richard Mabey, *Birds Britannica* (London: Chatto & Windus, 2005), p. 288.
2. https://app.bto.org/birdfacts/results/bob18820.htm
3. John Clare, 'Close where the milking maidens pass', in *John Clare's Birds*, edited by Eric Robinson and Richard Fitter (Oxford: Oxford University Press, 1982), p. 29, ll. 3–4, 13–14.
4. Paul F. Donald, et al., 'The Decline of the Corn Bunting', *British Birds*, vol. 87 (1994), 106–132, p. 125.
5. David Harper, 'Studies of West Palearctic Birds 194. Corn bunting Miliaria calandra', *British Birds*, vol. 88 (1995), p. 406.
6. https://app.bto.org/ring/countyrec/resultsall/rec18820all.htm.
7. Jo Holland, et al., 'Changes in Microgeographic Song Variation of the Corn Bunting Miliaria calandra', *Journal of Avian Biology*, vol. 27, no. 1 (1996), pp. 47–55.
8. Paul F. Donald, Jeremy D. Wilson and Michael Shepherd, 'The decline of the Corn Bunting', *British Birds*, 87 (March 1994), p. 117
9. Ibid., p. 54.
10. https://www.rspb.org.uk/globalassets/downloads/documents/conservation--sustainability/land-management-for-wildlife/land-management-for-wildlife---corn-bunting.pdf.
11. Mike J. Wareing, 'Farmland', in *Birdwatchers' Year* (Berkhamstead: T. & A. D. Poyser, 1973), p. 213.
12. J. A. Baker, *The Peregrine*, p. 15.
13. Wareing, p. 218.
14. Ibid.
15. Patrick Laurie, *Native* (Edinburgh: Birlinn, 2020), p. 142.
16. Cited in William Vaughan, *Gainsborough* (London: Thames and Hudson, 2002), p. 56.
17. https://www.gwct.org.uk/research/species/birds/grey-partridge/long-term-trends-in-grey-partridge-abundance/.
18. https://www.bto.org/about-bto/press-releases/tale-three-wagtails-familiar-species-decline.
19. https://www.bto.org/sites/default/files/shared_documents/gbw/associated_files/bird-table-73-mistle-thrush-species-focus.pdf.
20. https://www.bto.org/our-science/projects/bbs/research-conservation/cuckoo.
21. https://www.rspb.org.uk/our-work/conservation/projects/operation-turtle-dove.
22. Isabella Tree, *Wilding* (London: Picador, 2018), p. 194.
23. Ibid., p. 208.

24. *Wild Bird Populations in the UK, 1970–2018* (London: DEFRA, 2019), p. 37.
25. https://www.bto.org/about-bto/press-releases/turtle-dove-population-tailspin.
26. Aldo Leopold, *A Sand County Almanac* (Oxford: Oxford University Press, 1968), p. 48.
27. https://app.bto.org/birdtrends/species.jsp?s=linne
28. https://app.bto.org/birdtrends/species.jsp?s=skyla&year=2018.
29. Charles St John, *A Scottish Naturalist*, p. 84.
30. G. A. Tyler, et al., 'Survival and behaviour of Corncrake *Crex crex* chicks during the mowing of agricultural grasslands', *Bird Study*, vol. 45, no. 1 (1998), p. 35.
31. Valerie M. Thom, *Birds in Scotland* (Calton: T. & A. D. Poyser, 1986), p. 162.
32. https://www.rspb.org.uk/globalassets/downloads/documents/conservation--sustainability/hope-farm/Hope-Farm-Annual-Review.pdf.

6 Silence Descends

1. https://app.bto.org/birdfacts/results/bob12360.htm.
2. https://www.bto.org/our-science/projects/cuckoo-tracking-project/what-have-we-learnt.
3. Ibid.
4. Anonymous, 'Cuckoo', *The Poetry of Birds*, edited by Simon Armitage and Tim Dee (London: Viking, 2009), p. 117, ll. 1–2.
5. Ibid., ll. 10–12 and 13–14.
6. https://app.bto.org/birdfacts/results/bob7950.htm.
7. https://app.bto.org/birdtrends/species.jsp?year=2019&s=swift.
8. Lars Svensson, et al., *Collins Bird Guide* (London: Collins, 1999), p. 292.
9. Gordon Hamlin, *Our Birds Month by Month* (London: The Kingsgate Press, 1946), p. 63.
10. Ibid., pp. 65–6.
11. https://www.nasa.gov/audience/forstudents/k-4/home/F_Planet_Seasons.html.

Nightjar

1. R. W. Forrester, I. J. Andrews, et al., *The Birds of Scotland: Volume 2* (Aberlady: The Scottish Ornithologist's Club, 2007), pp. 932–3.

7 Fluctuations

1. https://www.bbc.co.uk/news/uk-scotland-south-scotland-52502075.
2. Richard Fox, et al., 'The State of the UK's Butterflies 2015', Butterfly Conservation (2015), p. 6.
3. John Keats, 'Ode to Psyche', *Romanticism: An Anthology*, edited by Duncan Wu (Malden: Blackwell, 2006), pp. 1393–1394, l. 35.
4. Trevor Beebee, *Climate Change and British Wildlife*, p. 91.
5. Ibid.
6. Jeremy Thomas and Richard Lewington, *The Butterflies of Britain & Ireland* (Dorset: British Wildlife Publishing, 2010), p. 5.
7. Michael McCarthy, *The Moth Snowstorm* (New York: New York Review of Books, 2015), p. 162.
8. Sibylle Rahlenbeck and Jochen Utikal, 'The oak processionary moth: a new health hazard?', *British Journal of General Practice*, vol. 65 (2015), p. 435.
9. Emer O'Connell, et al., 'Health effects of exposure to setae of oak processionary moth larvae: systematic review', Public Health England (2015), p. 7.
10. Nicolas Meurisse, et al., 'Natural History of the Oak Processionary Moth, *Thaumetopoea processionea*', in *Processionary Moths and Climate Change: An Update*, edited by Alain Roques (Dordrecht: Springer, 2015), p. 55.
11. Margaret Vickery, 'Butterflies as indicators of climate change', *Scientific Progress* (2008), vol. 91, no. 2, p. 197.
12. Richard Fox, et al., *The State of Britain's Larger Moths 2021*, Butterfly Conservation (2021), p. 2.
13. Daniel T. C. Cox, et al., 'Global variation in diurnal asymmetry in temperature, cloud cover, specific humidity and precipitation and its association with leaf area index', *Global Change Biology* (2020), p. 2.
14. Ibid., pp. 5 and 11.

Soprano Pipistrelle

1. https://www.bats.org.uk/about-bats/flight-food-and-echolocation.

8 The Illusion of Wildness

1. Mark Pollitt, et al., 'Dragonflies & Damselflies in SW Scotland', South West Scotland Environmental Information Centre (2019), p. 39.
2. John Buchan, *The Thirty-Nine Steps* (Ware: Wordsworth Editions, 1996), p. 38.

3. Steve Brooks, et al., *Field Guide to the Dragonflies & Damselflies of Great Britain and Ireland* (Oxford: British Wildlife Publishing, 2014), p. 148.

4. Filipe Dantas-Torres, 'Climate change, biodiversity, ticks and tick-borne diseases: the butterfly effect', *International Journal for Parasitology: Parasites and Wildlife*, vol. 4, (2015), p. 456.

5. Taal Levi, et al., 'Accelerated phenology of blacklegged ticks under climate warming', *Philosophical Transactions of the Royal Society B*, vol. 370 (2015), pp. 1–8.

6. Lisa I. Couper, et al., 'Impact of prior and projected climate change on US Lyme disease incidence', ll. 536–7, https://www.biorxiv.org/content/10.1101/2020.01.31.929380v2.full.pdf.

7. Robert Burns, 'Song Composed in August', in *The Works of Robert Burns* (Hertfordshire: Wordsworth Editions, 1994), pp. 357–8, l. 2.

8. Robert Burns, 'Verses on the destruction of the woods near Drumlanrig', in ibid., pp. 255–7, l. 48.

9. https://www.undiscoveredscotland.co.uk/thornhill/mortoncastle/index.html.

10. https://www.leadminingmuseum.co.uk/education-and-resources/.

11. https://www.drumlanrigcastle.co.uk/field-sports/game-shooting/.

12. https://raptorpersecutionscotland.wordpress.com/2012/10/09/golden-eagle-found-shot-critically-injured-on-scottish-grouse-moor/.

13. https://raptorpersecutionscotland.wordpress.com/2019/12/09/hen-harrier-found-shot-two-others-disappear-all-on-scottish-grouse-moors/.

14. John H. Salter, *Bird Life Throughout the Year* (London: The Swarthmore Press, 1917), pp. 187–8.

15. Ibid., p. 188.

16. Gordon Hamlin, *Our Birds Month by Month*, p. 85.

17. https://www.esquire.com/lifestyle/a4310/the-crack-up/.

Wasp Spider

1. W. S. Bristowe, *The World of Spiders* (London: Collins, 1976), p. 251.

2. Sabrina Kumschick, et al., 'Rapid spread of the wasp spider *Argiope bruennichi* across Europe: a consequence of climate change?', *Climatic Change*, vol. 109 (2011), p. 325.

9 Ghosts of Summer Future

1. https://www.bbc.co.uk/news/science-environment-51713172.

2. https://www.bbc.co.uk/news/science-environment-52877912.

Notes

3. All Met Office data taken from here: https://www.metoffice.gov.uk/weather/learn-about/past-uk-weather-events.

4. https://www.theguardian.com/world/2020/nov/05/arctic-time-capsule-from-2018-washes-up-in-ireland-as-polar-ice-melts.

5. Aldo Leopold, *Round River: From the Journals of Aldo Leopold* (Oxford: Oxford University Press, 1993), p. 165.

6. https://www.spamzine.co.uk/post/review-marine-objects---some-language-by-suzannah-v-evans.

7. https://www.narcissisticabuserehab.com/wp-content/uploads/2020/02/On-Narcissism-Sigmund-Freud.pdf p.16.

8. Timothy Morton, 'The Dark Ecology of Elegy', in *The Oxford Handbook of the Elegy*, edited by Karen Weisman (Oxford: Oxford University Press, 2010), p. 255.

9. John F. Burton, *Birds and Climate Change* (London: Christopher Helm, 1995), p. 307.

10. Amitav Ghosh, *The Great Derangement* (Chicago, University of Chicago Press, 2016), p. 9.

11. Mary Robinson, *Climate Justice* (London: Bloomsbury, 2019), p. 120.

12. https://www.greenpeace.org/canada/en/story/3138/everything-you-need-to-know-about-the-tar-sands-and-how-they-impact-you/.

13. bell hooks, *Teaching to Transgress* (New York: Routledge, 1994), p. 64.

14. Barry Lopez, *About This Life* (London: The Harvill Press, 1999), p. 135.

15. Jenny Offill, *Weather* (London: Granta, 2020), p. 133.

16. Leopold, p. 165.

Index

Index

Index